THE WAY PEOPLE LIVE

Life on an Everest Expedition

Titles in The Way People Live series include:

THE WAY
PEOPLE
LIVE

Life on an Everest Expedition

by
Patricia D. Netzley

Lucent Books, P.O. Box 289011, San Diego, CA 92198-9011

To Sarah, the mountaineer of the family

Library of Congress Cataloging-in-Publication Data

Netzley, Patricia D.
  Life on a Everest expedition / Patricia D. Netzley.
    p. cm. — (The way people live)
Includes bibliographical references (p.) and index.
  ISBN 1-56006-792-6 (alk. paper)
  1. Mountaineering expeditions—Everest, Mount (China and Nepal)—
Juvenile literature. 2. Everest, Mount (China and Nepal)—Description and
travel—Juvenile literature. [1. Mountaineering. 2. Everest, Mount (China and
Nepal)] I. Title. II. Series.
  GV199.44.E85 N48 2001
  796.52'2'095496—dc21

                                                        00-010971

Copyright 2001 by Lucent Books, Inc., P.O. Box 289011, San Diego, California
92198-9011

Printed in the U.S.A.

Contents

Discovering the Humanity in Us All

Books in The Way People Live series focus on groups of people in a wide variety of circumstances, settings, and time periods. Some books focus on different cultural groups, others, on people in a particular historical time period, while others cover people involved in a specific event. Each book emphasizes the daily routines, personal and historical struggles, and achievements of people from all walks of life.

To really understand any culture, it is necessary to strip the mind of the common notions we hold about groups of people. These stereotypes are the archenemies of learning. It does not even matter whether the stereotypes are positive or negative; they are confining and tight. Removing them is a challenge that's not easily met, as anyone who has ever tried it will admit. Ideas that do not fit into the templates we create are unwelcome visitors—ones we would prefer remain quietly in a corner or forgotten room.

The cowboy of the Old West is a good example of such confining roles. The cowboy was courageous, yet soft-spoken. His time (it is always a he, in our template) was spent alternatively saving a rancher's daughter from certain death on a runaway stagecoach, or shooting it out with rustlers. At times, of course, he was likely to get a little crazy in town after a trail drive, but for the most part, he was the epitome of inner strength. It is disconcerting to find out that the cowboy is human, even a bit childish. Can it really be true that cowboys would line up to help the cook on the trail drive grind coffee, just hoping he would give them a little stick of peppermint candy that came with the coffee shipment? The idea of tough cowboys vying with one another to help "Coosie" (as they called their cooks) for a bit of candy seems silly and out of place.

So is the vision of Eskimos playing video games and watching MTV, living in prefab housing in the Arctic. It just does not fit with what "Eskimo" means. We are far more comfortable with snow igloos and whale blubber, harpoons and kayaks.

Although the cultures dealt with in Lucent's The Way People Live series are often historically and socially well known, the emphasis is on the personal aspects of life. Groups of people, while unquestionably affected by their politics and their governmental structures, are more than those institutions. How do people in a particular time and place educate their children? What do they eat? And how do they build their houses? What kinds of work do they do? What kinds of games do they enjoy? The answers to these questions bring these cultures to life. People's lives are revealed in the particulars and only by knowing the particulars can we understand these cultures' will to survive and their moments of weakness and greatness.

This is not to say that understanding politics does not help to understand a culture. There is no question that the Warsaw ghetto, for example, was a culture that was brought about by the politics and social ideas of Adolf

Hitler and the Third Reich. But the Jews who were crowded together in the ghetto cannot be understood by the Reich's politics. Their life was a day-to-day battle for existence, and the creativity and methods they used to prolong their lives is a vital story of human perseverance that would be denied by focusing only on the institutions of Hitler's Germany. Knowing that children as young as five or six outwitted Nazi guards on a daily basis, that Jewish policemen helped the Germans control the ghetto, that children attended secret schools in the ghetto and even earned diplomas—these are the things that reveal the fabric of life, that can inspire, intrigue, and amaze.

Books in The Way People Live series allow both the casual reader and the student to see humans as victims, heroes, and onlookers. And although humans act in ways that can fill us with feelings of sorrow and revulsion, it is important to remember that "hero," "predator," and "victim" are dangerous terms. Heaping undue pity or praise on people reduces them to objects, and strips them of their humanity.

Seeing the Jews of Warsaw only as victims is to deny their humanity. Seeing them only as they appear in surviving photos, staring at the camera with infinite sadness, is limiting, both to them and to those who want to understand them. To an object of pity, the only appropriate response becomes "Those poor creatures!" and that reduces both the quality of their struggle and the depth of their despair. No one is served by such two-dimensional views of people and their cultures.

With this in mind, The Way People Live series strives to flesh out the traditional, two-dimensional views of people in various cultures and historical circumstances. Using a wide variety of primary quotations—the words not only of the politicians and government leaders, but of the real people whose lives are being examined—each book in the series attempts to show an honest and complete picture of a culture removed from our own by time or space.

By examining cultures in this way, the reader will notice not only the glaring differences from his or her own culture, but also will be struck by the similarities. For indeed, people share common needs—warmth, good company, stability, and affirmation from others. Ultimately, seeing how people really live, or have lived, can only enrich our understanding of ourselves.

"A Fever in the Blood"

At 29,028 feet, Mount Everest in Asia's Himalayan mountain range is the tallest mountain on Earth. Someone standing on the peak has an unblocked view of the horizon in all directions. Below are the countries of Nepal and Tibet, and 100 miles away is Darjeeling, India, where the first expeditions to climb Everest began.

Only fourteen other peaks in the world even come close to Everest's height, and most of them are also in the Himalayas. These peaks are known as "the Eights" because they are all more than 26,240 feet—or 8,000 meters—high. Their bad weather, heavy snow, and glacial ice present formidable challenges to even the best mountaineers. But more importantly, their altitudes are so high that no human being can survive on them for very long because, above 8,000 meters, there is not enough oxygen in the air to support life for more than five days. And the only way to survive even that long is by making a gradual ascent so that the human body has time to adjust to changes in air pressure and the low oxygen levels that occur as a person climbs higher and higher. Yet even as the body makes this gradual adjustment, any physical exertion is extremely debilitating.

Fame and Glory

Nonetheless, roughly four thousand people have attempted to climb to Everest's peak—an activity known as summitting—and about 1000 have succeeded. The reasons why so many people have been compelled to climb Everest vary. Prior to 1953, when Sir Edmund Hillary and Tenzing Norgay became the first men to reach Everest's peak, men struggled to summit because they wanted the fame and glory that came with conquering the seemingly unconquerable. The British particularly wanted the honor of putting the first man on the peak; in fact, they sponsored Hillary and Norgay's successful 1953 expedition.

After this expedition, mountaineers continued to vie for a series of "firsts": the first American to reach Everest's summit, for example; the first person to reach it from a new route; the first woman to reach it; or the first solo climber to reach it. Mountaineers unable to find a particular "first" to tackle summitted to beat records, trying to climb Everest the fastest or to become the oldest or youngest climber to reach the peak. Some even attempted to become the first person to summit all of the Eights—a goal achieved by mountaineer Reinhold Messner in 1986.

Personal Satisfaction

Messner claimed that he, unlike many others, climbed for more than just fame and glory. He went for the challenge, for personal satisfaction, and to spend time alone. He found great joy in climbing Everest despite its dangers, but he often had difficulty getting nonmountaineers to believe this. In several interviews he expressed frustration when people questioned his sanity for participating in such a dangerous sport.

Other mountain climbers have voiced similar frustrations. For example, mountaineer Frank S. Smythe said that he faced undue criticism for trying to climb Everest in 1933. In his book *The Spirit of the Hills,* he defended his desire to reach the peak, saying,

Some people achieve happiness best by seeking out the wildest and most inaccessible corners of the earth, and there subjugating their bodies to discomfort and even to peril, in search of an ideal which goes by the simple word "discovery," discovery not only of physical objects but of themselves. To condemn another's ideals, however foolish they may seem at first sight, unless there is something inherently evil in them, is to stand yourself condemned of a retrograde narrow-mindedness.[1]

Glaciers on Mt. Everest, the tallest mountain on Earth.

A Man of "Sheer Dash"

Some men had more drive than most to ascend Everest's peak. George Leigh Mallory, who disappeared on Everest in 1924, was just such a man. According to James Ramsey Ullman in his book *Kingdom of Adventure*, the photographer on Mallory's 1924 expedition, John Noel, later said of him,

"Mallory was no ordinary man. . . . For sheer dash there was no one to touch this young climber. He applied himself to the task, which might have appalled most other men by its danger and magnitude, with indomitable energy and will. . . . With his physical strength he had a vivid imagination and a great heart. He seemed to live in a realm remote from everyday life. It could be seen that he had great imagination and ideals. He was stubborn to a degree; and his ideas were, perhaps, lacking in flexibility; but yet in another sense this same rigidity contributed to the strength of that determination which caused him to push through with dauntless energy any enterprise he might take up. . . . How this mountain obsessed him! He threw his whole body and soul into the fight against her. He seemed always as if he were measuring and calculating. Yet I always felt in my own acquaintance with him that some strange fatalism overshadowed his ambition. I could

George Leigh Mallory (left) and fellow climber on a jagged edge of Mt. Everest.

notice that he was always trying to convince himself that he could beat the mountain but at the same time he seemed to show a consciousness somehow or other that the mountain held the mastery."

But whereas nonmountaineers often puzzle over why someone would want to climb a peak as dangerous as Everest, mountaineers do not consider it folly at all. As Danish mountaineer Lene Gammelgaard, who successfully summitted Everest in 1996, once explained, all mountaineers share the same feelings about their sport: "It's . . . obvious how uniformly we [mountaineers] think, express ourselves and are driven by recognizable inner forces. In 'our universe' we are the norm, and the others are those that do not understand. We don't ask why we do it. Nor do we admire. That's just the way it is."[2]

For this reason, all mountaineers, despite whether they long to reach Everest's peak, understand the mountain's spell. For instance, geologist and mountaineer Noel Odell, who unsuccessfully searched for missing climbers

George Mallory and Andrew Irvine during a 1924 expedition, later said that despite his friends' deaths he continued to find the mountain's peak compelling: "There seemed to be something alluring in that towering presence. I was almost fascinated. I realized that he who approached close must ever be led on, and oblivious of all obstacles seek to reach that most sacred and highest place of all."[3]

Fears and Obsessions

Of course, everyone who attempts to summit Everest is aware of the mountain's dangers. Some mountaineers even struggle with fear while climbing. For example, Messner says, "Fear [on Everest] is a constant companion. . . . You can't live life fully without it. When things get critical, your fear becomes even more intense. . . . If you remain conscious that death is part of life, you cannot suppress your basic fear of falling, or of being overwhelmed by the weather."[4]

Others put their fears aside when they climb, and a few claim to have no fear at all. In the latter category is Russian mountaineer Anatoli Boukreev, who received awards for his skills and for bravery in rescuing several people during a 1996 Everest disaster. Boukreev once said,

"Honestly, I do not experience fear in the mountains. On the contrary . . . I feel my shoulders straightening, squaring, like the birds as they straighten their wings. I enjoy the freedom and the altitude. It is only when I return to life below that I feel the world's weight on my shoulders."[5]

Boukreev died on another Himalayan "Eight," Annapurna, in an avalanche in December 1997. But even the deaths of experienced mountaineers do not deter people who want to climb Everest. As Tenzing Norgay once explained, the desire to reach the mountain's peak can become an obsession that is impossible to dismiss. In his book *Tiger of the Snows* he writes, "When I am on Everest I can think of nothing else. I want only to go on, farther and farther. It is a dream, a need, a fever in the blood."[6]

Most of the people who have climbed Everest speak of their obsession with the mountain, and all share memories of a difficult, dangerous experience. Some have come away pleased with this experience while others regret it. But in either case, they typically learn a lot about themselves while on the mountain. Among mountaineers it is said that Everest challenges a climber in a way no other mountain ever does or ever can, and joining an Everest expedition is a way for people to test themselves both physically and psychologically.

Deciding When and How to Climb

People who attempt to climb Everest rarely do so alone. Many things can go wrong during a climb, and having a partner ensures that someone will be there to offer help during a crisis. Consequently, most mountaineers who want to climb Everest look for an expedition they can join.

An expedition is a group of people whose goal is to put at least one member on the peak. Prior to 1953 no expedition had managed to achieve this goal. Today, however, many expeditions put most of their members on the peak. This success depends largely on careful planning. Expedition organizers must make many decisions before embarking on their trip to Everest, and each of these decisions affects the type of experience they will have on the mountain.

When to Climb

One of the first decisions is when to climb Everest. Due to a wind current called the jet stream, there are only two times of year when weather conditions for a climb are optimal. There are four major jet streams that move across the surface of the earth; one of them usually blows across Everest nonstop at twenty-six thousand feet, bringing moisture from subtropical regions to this altitude. This moisture in turn creates storm after storm near the peak. However, for three to ten days in the spring—usually in May—the jet stream shifts to a point far above Everest, which in turn eliminates the storms at

the summit. The jet stream again shifts upward in the fall, but this storm-free period is less reliable, and the temperatures on the mountain are much colder at this time. Therefore, few mountaineers climb in the fall, and it is spring that is dubbed climbing season in Nepal and Tibet.

Even during the spring, however, many expeditions have failed because of bad weather. These include large expeditions in 1933, 1935, 1936, and 1938, during which not a single man reached the peak. During these years the spring storm-free period on the mountain was short or nonexistent. Conversely, in spring 1995 the north side of Everest had a stretch of storm-free weather that lasted approximately two weeks, and eighty-eight climbers were able to reach the mountain's peak. Never before had the north side experienced such a calm period. In fact, the weather is so difficult on north Everest that up until 1995 only sixty-six mountaineers had ever managed to reach the top of the mountain via that side.

Why Good Weather is Important

The reason why storms bring failure is because they are unusually severe on Everest. Temperatures can easily drop twenty degrees in twenty minutes. Static in the air can cause radio communication to fail. Even worse, visibility can drop to zero, leaving climbers unable to find their way. Amateur climber Beck Weathers describes a storm on Everest's south side in 1996:

The storm began as a low, distant growl, then rapidly formed into a howling white fog laced with ice pellets. It hurtled up Mount Everest to engulf us in minutes. We couldn't see as far as our feet. A person standing next to you just vanished in the roaring whiteout. Wind speeds that night would exceed seventy knots. The ambient temperature fell to sixty below zero.[7]

Storms are typically accompanied by winds so strong—in some cases, over 80 miles per hour—that they can knock climbers off their feet and lash exposed skin hard enough to make

Failed radio communications, extremely high winds, and sudden drops in temperature contribute to the climbers' failure to reach Everest's summit.

Deciding When and How to Climb

it bleed. Even mountaineers in tents are not safe from the fury of such winds. British mountaineer George Finch, who was part of the 1922 expedition on Everest's north side, offers perhaps the best description of a battle with winds in a camp at 25,500 feet:

Terrific gusts tore at our tent with such ferocity that . . . [the tent was] frequently lifted up off the ground. On these occasions [the] combined efforts [of three men] were needed to keep the tent down and prevent its being blown away. Although we had blocked up the few very small openings in the tent to the best of our powers, long before midnight we were all thickly covered in the fine frozen snow that somehow or other was blown in upon

Good visibility is extremely important to a successful Mt. Everest climbing expedition.

The Massive Himalayas

Mountaineers flying over the Himalayas on their way to Nepal are overwhelmed by the sight of the massive mountains. Woodrow Wilson Sayre, en route to his own Everest assault in 1962, describes his first glimpse of the range in his book *Four Against Everest*.

Mt. Everest is a part of the great Himalayan mountain range.

"It was exciting to see [the mountains], but also a bit scary. The whole Himalayan range is like a giant storm wave surging out of the north towards the Indian plains. The wave crests over five miles up in the air. Think of the highest peaks in [the] Rocky Mountains; they will have a little scattered frosting of ice and snow on their highest crags. Now go a half mile vertically straight up and you will have just gotten to the *lower* part of the snow line on the Himalayas. Then imagine two more vertical miles of ice and snow and glacier stretching on up from this snow line. Now maybe you can imagine a bit the unbelievable Himalayas. . . . I suddenly felt how puny our preparations were. How could we hope to surmount any of these giants? It seemed absurd."

us, insinuating its way into sleeping-bags and clothing.

Sleep was out of the question. We dared not relax our vigilance, for our strength was needed to hold the tent down and to keep the flaps of the door, stripped of their fastenings by a gust that had caught us unawares, from being torn open. We fought for our lives, realizing that once the wind got our little shelter into its ruthless grip, it must inevitably be hurled, with us inside it, . . . thousands of feet below.[8]

Because good weather is vital to a successful summit, most mountaineers plan their expedition so that they will be ready to climb to twenty-six thousand feet when the jet stream lifts. They travel to the mountain prior to those few days in May and remain at lower altitudes until the right moment arrives. During this waiting period, any storms they encounter are usually milder than those nearer the peak.

Which Route to Take

In addition to planning when to climb, expedition organizers must decide in advance which route to take both to the base of the mountain and up its slopes. Prior to 1951 all expeditions had to travel to Everest through Tibet rather than Nepal because the Nepalese government refused to allow any foreigners into its country. Meanwhile, the Tibetans permitted only the British, who entered Tibet from India, to climb Everest. Today, however, expeditions can travel through either Nepal or Tibet. Those who choose to begin on the Nepalese side of Everest's base will be climbing up the mountain's south face; those who begin on the Tibetan side will be climbing up the north face.

The northern and southern routes up the mountain do not present mountaineers with the same type of terrain, however. As Tenzing Norgay says, "To climb a mountain from a different side is almost like climbing a different mountain."[9] In the case of Everest, the most important distinction has to do with where the most difficult terrain is located. On the north side of the mountain, the hardest part of the climb is near the peak; on the south side, the reverse is true.

Organizers of the earliest British Everest expeditions thought the climb on the north side offered them the best chance of being first on the peak. Their reasoning had to do with the large amount of heavy supplies they brought with them. They knew it would be easier to carry these supplies to and partway up the north side than the south, and this fit with their method of trying to reach the peak—or, as they called it, attacking or assaulting the summit.

The British typically established a series of camps up the mountain, moving supplies closer and closer to the peak. Their last camp would be just below the most difficult part of the climb on the north side. Pairs of mountaineers could then assault the summit in succession, beginning from that highest camp, without carrying heavy supplies.

But even with careful planning, each British assault on the summit from the north failed. Eventually expedition organizers realized that the last part of the climb on the north side was just too difficult. By the time their mountaineers reached the last few hundred feet of their ascent, not only were they tired from having spent several days climbing up the mountain, but they were also dealing with the rigors of exerting themselves at high altitude with low oxygen levels.

In contrast, the climb on the south side of Everest was easiest nearest the peak; experienced mountaineers found it manageable even when they were tired, providing no storms were present. Consequently, it is no coincidence that the first successful assault on the summit took place via the southern route.

Since then, the majority of individuals attempting to climb Everest have chosen the southern route, believing it maximizes their chances of successfully reaching the peak. Of the roughly one thousand people who have attained this goal, fewer than seventy have climbed via the north. In fact, since the first mountaineers started climbing, only about seven hundred have even tried the northern route. In the case of modern expeditions, however, a roughly equal number take both routes. In 1996, for example, out of the thirty expeditions on the mountain during climbing season, fourteen took the northern route and sixteen the southern route.

However, there is a significant difference between the types of expeditions that take each route. Today most of the expeditions using the southern route are intended for amateur climbers, while those on the northern route are for experienced mountaineers. The reason for this has to do with the climbers' goals. Amateurs usually go to Everest with only one intent: reaching the top. Experienced mountaineers want to reach the top of the mountain too, but they also usually want the most challenging climb possible, and this is what the north side offers.

Two other reasons why people choose the northern route despite its difficulty are cost and availability. Nepal and Tibet each allow only a certain number of people to climb the mountain per year, issuing climbing permits to expeditions on a first-come, first-served basis. Permits issued by Nepal for climbs up the south side are in higher demand and are also more expensive than Tibetan permits. As of 1996, a Nepalese permit cost ten thousand dollars per mountaineer, with a seventy thousand dollar minimum. In other words, an expedition must pay for at least seven permits even if it does not have seven mountaineers. In contrast, the Chinese government, which currently controls Tibet, charges only fifteen thousand dollars for an entire expedition, regardless of size. However, an expedition choosing the northern route is also required to pay the government to transport its members and supplies to the base of the mountain. These fees vary according to the size of the expedition, but even with this expense, the northern route is still cheaper.

Taxing Expedition Supplies

In budgeting for supplies, expedition organizers must consider not only their purchase cost but also how much money it will take to get them into Nepal. In his book *Four Against Everest*, Woodrow Wilson Sayre complains about taxes and restrictions on mountaineering supplies instituted by the Nepalese government in 1962.

"As of the first of the year there was a new schedule of [import] taxes on every item of equipment. . . . The [American] embassy and various mountain groups were protesting, but there was nothing really that could be done, at least at the moment. These new taxes varied from 10 percent to 90 percent, with the average around 60 percent. There was a crazy-quilt pattern of classification set up, and each classification had its own level of tax. Thus, plastics were taxed at 80 percent, cheese 30 percent, meat 50 percent. Shoes, clothing, ironware, toilet paper, hats—every item had its separate tax. We were not allowed to know the rates in advance, so it became a guessing game. Do you classify a plastic-handled knife as 'ironware' or as 'plastic'? We guessed 'plastic,' thinking it would have a lower tax. Wrong. Plastics are taxed at 80 percent, ironware at only 60 percent. . . . The climax . . . came after two solid days of meticulous, item-by-item examination of our goods. There was a new rule, previously unknown to us, or indeed to anyone, that all beef products were to be confiscated due to religious scruples. [The Nepalese believe it is wrong to eat cattle.] Luckily our meat bars had no large labels saying 'Beef' on them. . . . The loss of these essential provisions . . . would certainly finish [our expedition]."

How to Fund an Expedition

To pay for permits, gear, and supplies, expedition organizers must decide whether they want to become a sponsored expedition or a commercial one. Sponsored expeditions do not usually charge their mountaineers a fee to participate in the climb. Instead, they raise money from people, government agencies, and organizations that want to support mountaineering efforts. The first British expeditions were funded by the British government and mountaineering clubs. Funding for sponsored American expeditions has most typically come from businesses, individuals, and government and university grants. The 1963 American expedition, for example, cost $405,000; its funding came from the National Geographic Society and several magazines as well as grants and private donations. In addition, much of the expedition's gear was donated by manufacturers.

In contrast, commercial expeditions charge each mountaineer on the expedition a large fee —which not only covers all expenses but also provides organizers with a profit. Commercial expeditions on the north side of Everest generally charge between eighteen and twenty-four thousand dollars per person; those on the south charge between thirty and sixty-five thousand dollars per person. Therefore, in most cases only wealthy people participate in commercial expeditions; however, sometimes an individual mountaineer who does not have enough money for the trip will solicit private donations. This is most common with someone attempting a "first." For instance, private donations helped Lene Gammelgaard become the first Danish woman to climb Everest, a feat she accomplished in 1996.

Guides from the Mountain Madness Guided Expedition in 1996 assemble with expedition members for a group photo.

Yaks help carry supplies to Base Camp.

The idea of an individual mountaineer having to pay to climb Everest is relatively new. Prior to the 1980s there was no such thing as a commercial expedition because people believed Everest expeditions were only for highly trained athletes. Then, in 1985, a millionaire named Dick Bass paid American mountaineer David Breashears to escort him up the mountain. Bass was not only an amateur climber but also—at age fifty-five—the oldest man to summit Everest. These facts changed people's view of how difficult it was to climb the mountain. Summitting Everest suddenly seemed attainable to anyone with enough money to hire an experienced mountaineer as a guide. Demand for Everest "tickets to the top" increased, and dozens of commercial expedition companies sprang up in response. Most of them currently operate on the south side of Everest, following the same path as Sir Edmund Hillary's successful 1953 expedition.

How Many People to Include

Because commercial expeditions are funded by the mountaineers themselves, these expeditions can have as many members as are willing to pay their way, providing the required number of climbing permits is available. Mountaineers have criticized the organizers of some commercial expeditions for including more people than is safe just so they can maximize profits. When there are too many amateur mountaineers on an expedition, professional guides cannot properly help them with any problems they might encounter.

For example, in 1996 the Adventure Consultants Guided Expedition had ten paying

Sherpa guide (right) with tourist. Sherpas live in the highland valleys of Nepal and act as tour guides for people who wish to explore Mt. Everest.

climbers but only three guides, and the Mountain Madness Guided Expedition had nine paying clients with three guides. Each expedition had around a dozen other workers as well, but they were used primarily to set up camps and did not help the clients climb. As a result, when a storm hit the mountain, the clients did not have enough help getting back to camp and five people died. Meanwhile, the Alpine Ascents International Guided Expedition had three guides for three clients, with no deaths.

There were several sponsored expeditions on the mountain that year as well, and they too had no deaths. Unconcerned with making a profit, sponsored expeditions usually take only the number of people that organizers believe is sensible and safe. There has been some disagreement, however, over exactly what this number should be. Eric Shipton, who led British expeditions in the 1930s, argued that expeditions should have no more than six mountaineers because a larger group would not have the trust and closeness necessary to work well as a team. Nonetheless, the early British expeditions typically had about a dozen mountaineers because their organizers believed that this number would increase the odds that at least one person would make it to the top of the mountain.

In addition to mountaineers, expeditions have support personnel such as porters and herders to help set up camp. Porters carry gear on their backs to the base of the mountain, and herders drive pack animals carrying gear too heavy for the porters. The primary animal used by the herders is the yak, which resembles a water buffalo, although donkeys are included as well. Some expeditions have needed as many as four hundred animals and nine hundred porters to get supplies to the base of Everest. Once there, the expedition establishes a campsite that is always referred to as Base Camp, whether on the north side or the south side of the mountain.

The Sherpas

Once Base Camp is set up, the porters, herders, and animals are sent on their way, but other workers remain. Many of these are Sherpas, native people from an ethnic group indigenous to Tibet. Centuries ago, their ancestors migrated east into the highland valleys of Nepal—in fact, the name *Sherpa* means "Man from the East"—over perhaps the same route now used by traders who visit both countries. Because of this ancestral connection, Sherpa and Tibetan religious beliefs, customs, clothing, and language are very similar. But there is one fundamental difference between the two groups. The Sherpas have, as a whole, dedicated their lives to helping Westerners climb Himalayan mountains.

Sherpas have been on every major Everest expedition since the first British assaults on the peak; today, three thousand Sherpas currently live near Everest, with the majority of them offering support to Himalayan climbers. Some work as porters, cooks, or herders, but most act as high-altitude climbers, because they have the ability to ascend mountains proficiently and

Sherpa Generosity

One of the things that Sherpas are most noted for is their generosity. Sherry B. Ortner summarizes the activities that have led to the Sherpas' good reputation in her book *Life and Death on Mount Everest: Sherpas and Himalayan Mountaineering.*

"Sherpas have given up their oxygen if sahib [the Western mountaineer] needed it; given up their blankets or sleeping bags or waterproof gear when there was not enough; slept outside of the tent when the sahibs had taken up all the room inside; spent hours rubbing a sahib's hands or feet to prevent frostbite; stayed behind to help a slower climber when all the other sahibs had rushed off; carried sick and wounded sahibs twice their size down the mountain; voluntarily made extra trips for supplies; climbed part way back up a mountain with hot tea to meet a successful summit party coming down and to relieve them of their packs; and more. In almost every case the Sherpas *offered* to do these extra things without being asked. While at some level they may have felt they had little choice, the offers still seemed genuinely ungrudging and communicated striking generosity. . . . These acts of generosity in turn shaded into acts of outright heroism in an accident or a crisis. Sherpas on expeditions have made extraordinary efforts, going out under terrible conditions, when everyone else was exhausted, to try to rescue stranded climbers. In some cases they died trying."

with less physical effort than most Westerners. Early Everest expeditions were the first to recognize these unique skills, hiring at least thirty Sherpas to test and mark routes and establish high-altitude camps. Sherpas continue to perform these tasks today.

Sherpa Abilities

The Sherpas' proficiency in working high on Everest comes from their vast experience. Because they participate in so many expeditions, they have many opportunities to learn about Himalayan terrain, climbing techniques, dangers, and weather patterns. Their advice has therefore proved extremely valuable to Western mountaineers. In addition, because Sherpas live and work year-round in the Himalayas, their bodies have adapted to the higher altitudes there. This means that while summitting Everest, Sherpas move and breathe with greater ease than most people. Not only can they carry gear

up the mountain very efficiently, but they can also move quickly to rescue stranded climbers.

Tenzing Norgay was a Sherpa, and he attributed his successful 1953 summit largely to his physical advantages. He once said,

> I think it is perhaps true that I am more adapted to heights than most men; that I was born not only in, but *for*, the mountains. I climb with rhythm, and it is a natural thing for me. My hands, even in warm weather, are usually cold, and doctors have told me that my heartbeat is quite slow. The high places are my home. They are where I belong.[10]

Physicians who have studied the Sherpas have confirmed that their physical advantages are real and that they are passed down from one generation to the next. In addition, observers of the Sherpas note that these people have a culture that encourages them to endure a severe environment without complaint. Weak

The Sherpas and the British

The Sherpas on the first Everest expeditions generally got along well with their British employers. However, the British did not treat the Sherpas as equals, and this irritated some of them. In his book *Tiger of the Snows*, Sherpa Tenzing Norgay, who summitted with Sir Edmund Hillary, discusses his feelings.

"In all honesty, I would rather [go] to Everest with the Swiss. . . . This does not mean that I dislike the British. . . . But it is still true that the English in general are more reserved and formal than the men of most other countries whom I have known; and especially is this so, I think, with people not of

their own race. Perhaps this is because they have so long been rulers in the East, or perhaps it is only something in their own nature. But it is a thing which we Sherpas have had much chance to observe, since we have climbed, in recent years, with men of so many nations. With the Swiss and the French I had been treated as a comrade, an equal, in a way that is not possible for the British. They are kind men; they are brave; they are fair and just, always. But always, too, there is a line between them and the outsider, between sahib [master] and employee, and to such Easterners as we Sherpas, who have experienced the world of no-line, this can be a difficulty and a problem."

individuals are weeded out, so Sherpas learn not to show weakness. As Danish mountaineer Gammelgaard explains,

> Sherpas admire, respect true strength; it's probably deeply rooted in them—common sense under their life conditions. If a baby doesn't have sufficient strength, it dies young. To survive and live in this harsh environment demands stamina, and no one attempts to breast-feed and keep a child alive if it shows signs of weakness.[11]

Sherpas also generally have pleasant dispositions and enjoy hard work. These traits, along with their physical advantages, make them desirable additions to Everest expeditions. Moreover, Sherpas have always been fairly cheap labor. In 1935, Sherpas who worked at high altitudes earned only 35¢ a day. In 1963 they received approximately $1 a day. Today a Sherpa earns around $1,400 to $2,500 per two-month expedition. This does not seem like a lot to Western mountaineers, but it is a fortune in a region where most people earn only about $160 a year.

Once expedition organizers have determined how many Sherpas and other workers they need and can afford to include, they can calculate how many supplies they must take on their journey. Outfitting an expedition is a difficult task with many considerations, all complicated by the fact that weather can sometimes make an expedition last far longer than intended. Therefore, the early planning stages of an expedition are easy compared to what comes next.

Outfitting an Expedition

Aside from climbing the mountain itself, the most difficult part of an Everest expedition is deciding what to take along on the trip. This is partly because Everest offers nothing to sustain life. James Ramsey Ullman, the leader of the 1963 American expedition, explains:

> On Everest there is absolutely no possibility of living off the land. Food, tents, utensils, clothing, climbing gear, medicines, scientific instruments—literally *everything*—must first be transported for hundreds of miles across wild, inhospitable terrain and subsequently carried up the mountain itself to the high and inaccessible camps.[12]

Taking along too many supplies, however, can be as problematic as taking too few. In addition to carrying personal items and sleeping bags on their backs, mountaineers are often expected to carry part of an expedition's communal gear. If there are too many goods, the additional weight can cause exhaustion and physical injury. Consequently, mountaineers debate about what items are truly necessary for a climb. Nonetheless, certain generalities can be made about the supplies Everest expeditions need in order to have a successful summit.

Supplemental Oxygen

Most people believe that mountaineers must have supplemental oxygen to reach Everest's peak. As climbers go higher on the mountain and the atmosphere thins, their breathing becomes labored and their muscles inefficient. Breathing bottled oxygen alleviates this problem. As Dr. Thomas F. Hornbein, a member of the 1963 American Everest expedition, explains,

> The sheer necessity of oxygen for uphill movement at 29,000 feet is only too apparent to most Himalayan mountaineers. Beyond this, the use of oxygen increases the distance a climber can travel in a day and thereby ultimately shortens the time of his stay at very great heights. It adds immeasurably to his safety and clearness of judgment. . . . Without oxygen, each step at great heights is virtually a maximal effort; there is no reserve with which to face the unexpected.[13]

Thus, many expedition organizers consider oxygen tanks to be one of their first priorities when purchasing supplies, and they usually buy enough tanks to last their mountaineers for the entire climb, or at least for the part of the climb above twenty-six thousand feet. Some expedition leaders, however, buy only a few tanks for emergency purposes. This is because they believe it is unwise to rely on supplemental oxygen while on Everest.

They base this belief on two factors: the weight of oxygen tanks and their limited supply of air. Empty oxygen containers weigh roughly ten pounds, and full ones weigh a few pounds more. (In earlier times, full containers were four to six times heavier.) Since climbers usually carry more than one tank, this additional weight can hasten exhaustion during a day's climb. In addition, once a climber begins to rely on supplemental oxygen his or her body quickly becomes dependent on it; if a tank runs out of air and no replacement is available, the climber immediately becomes ill.

Because running out of supplemental air can make a mountaineer sick, expedition organizers who provide oxygen must calculate requirements carefully. Each person generally uses an oxygen flow rate of two to two and a half liters per minute, a rate that makes a modern-day canister of oxygen last about six hours. This means that a mountaineer on the southern route needs two oxygen canisters to make the

A climber sits among several tanks of oxygen. Most mountaineers consider supplemental oxygen a necessity for Everest climbs.

The Oxygen Apparatus

There are many different types of oxygen equipment, and many changes have been made in their design over the years. Advances in technology developed during World Wars I and II brought about lighter tanks and more efficient oxygen-delivery systems. Basically, however, Everest mountaineers have relied on a tank with an open-circuit system, which means that the oxygen device draws in outside air and enriches it with bottled oxygen. (A closed-delivery system uses nothing but bottled oxygen and recycles the air breathed by the user.) The typical open-circuit oxygen device consists of a container of pressurized oxygen, a pressure-reducing and flow-regulating device, and a tube that delivers oxygen to a collection chamber where it awaits each breath. The climber breathes the air through a mask with two valves, one to direct the air into the mouth for a breath and the other to direct the exhaled air outside of the mask. Ice sometimes forms on the mask where the climber's warm exhaled air meets the cold air on Everest; this makes exhalation harder for the mountaineer, who must stop occasionally to remove the ice.

twelve-hour climb from the highest campsite up to the summit and back down to a rocky area just below the summit. Sherpas store fresh oxygen canisters at this rocky spot so climbers can replace their empty tanks with full ones for their descent to camp.

Sometimes, however, climbers use up their tanks too quickly, usually because they increased the flow rate on their tanks to get more oxygen. A few people find themselves struggling to breathe at the regular rate, so they give themselves a richer oxygen mix. Climbers who do this run out of air too soon, and unless other mountaineers immediately give them fresh tanks, they will collapse and require rescue.

Some climbers also become overly dependent on using oxygen to sleep. At any altitude, the amount of oxygen in red blood cells drops during the night because of a sleeper's slower breathing rate. At high altitudes this can cause breathing to stop intermittently during sleep. The climber wakes up gasping for breath, falls back to sleep, and soon wakes with a gasp again. Using bottled oxygen prevents this problem. However, if mountaineers waste too many oxygen tanks on a good night's sleep, they might not have enough for a subsequent climb.

Food

Similarly, if climbers consume too much food, there will not be enough for later. Therefore, expedition organizers calculate food supplies carefully. Porters must bring enough food to Base Camp to last through any reasonable weather delays on the mountain yet not so much that it would be difficult to transport. As with oxygen, though, it is difficult to determine how much food each expedition member will consume per day.

Most expeditions choose foods they believe will be the easiest to transport and eat but will still offer enough calories for the demands of mountaineering. Climbers need more than six thousand calories per day—perhaps double that while exerting themselves during the last leg of the climb—with 50 to 70 percent of those calories coming from carbohydrates, 20 to 30 percent from proteins, and 20 to 30 percent from fats.

Because they can be transported easily, dried and tinned meats and canned milk have long been a favorite source of protein and fats on expeditions. Foods that provide carbohydrates include cereals, rice, pasta, crackers, bread, and granola. For a snack, the first British expedition members enjoyed scones, jams, and tea, just as they did at home. Modern climbers, however, typically carry protein bars or similar packaged foods instead. Since sugar is a good way to get extra calories and can provide an energy boost, many climbers also eat dried fruit, fruit bars, cookies, and chocolate.

Mountaineers eat the widest variety of foods at Base Camp because it is easiest for ex-peditions to transport goods there. In addition, Sherpas from local villages sometimes visit Base Camp to sell mountaineers items such as fresh eggs and Sherpa stew, which is made with yak meat and is seasoned with curry. As climbers go to campsites higher up the mountain, however, they have fewer food choices. They make simple meals themselves on special cookstoves or gas burners designed for use in tents. These meals must have a high water content because the human body often becomes dehydrated

Mountaineers eat together during an Everest expedition.

during a climb at high altitude. Dried soup powders mixed with water are a particular favorite, as are tea and drinks made from powdered beverage mixes. A drink made with powdered lemon juice mixed with sugar and water, for example, was the preferred choice of Sir Edmund Hillary at high campsites.

Since water freezes at high altitudes, climbers must melt snow in order to make their beverages. This takes a long time and, as mountaineer Reinhold Messner notes, "It is unbelievable how much snow one needs to get a bit of water."[14] It is also difficult to make beverages or soup truly hot because at high altitudes water boils at a lower temperature; in the highest camps on Everest, climbers can stick their hands in a pot of boiling water without burning themselves.

Water consumption is important at Base Camp as well. Lene Gammelgaard reports that

At high altitudes the skin becomes cracked and the body parched from dehydration.

most people there carry a thermos and a plastic flask. She explains why:

> After every meal, the Sherpas fill our containers with boiled water. The Thermos keeps my drinking water from freezing during the night, and I use the boiled water in the plastic flask to warm my feet at the beginning of the night. I'm meticulous about gulping down sufficient fluids—water, tea, juice and water, juice and more water—so I'm always waking up at night to drink and pee. Downing enough fluids helps you acclimatize [get used to the altitude] and is the best preventative measure you can take for altitude sickness.[15]

Medical Supplies

Some people get very sick at high altitudes, experiencing nausea, headaches, mental confusion, and other symptoms. Expedition organizers must therefore take along the proper medicines to treat these conditions. They must also be prepared to treat the broken bones, sprains, and frostbite injuries that are common in glacier climbing.

Frostbite results from the freezing of extremities, during which blood circulation stops and tissue dies. Severely frostbitten fingers and toes sometimes fall off on their own, but more often they have to be amputated once the victim is off the mountain. With mild cases, the afflicted limb can be saved if it is placed in warm water to thaw and is then dressed in an ointment of silver nitrate, which is also used to treat burns.

Additional medical supplies usually include surgical equipment, dental supplies, anesthetic supplies, lab equipment, immuniza-

tion equipment, and first-aid kits for each expedition member. As with food and oxygen, expedition organizers must carefully calculate the amount of medical supplies they will require. This amount varies depending on the size of the expedition, but it is not unusual for a large expedition to carry two hundred pounds of medical supplies and equipment to Base Camp.

The most frequently used medications on Everest, however, are cough medicines and anti-diarrhea medicines. Most climbers develop a mild to severe cough while on Everest due to the drier, thinner air. In severe cases, the cough can be so violent that it cracks ribs. Many mountaineers also develop diarrhea, usually as a result of eating unsanitary food in Nepal or Tibet prior to reaching Everest. Drinking river water during the trek to Base Camp can also cause diarrhea because it contains harmful microorganisms due to feces contamination.

Communication Equipment

In case of medical emergencies, radios and other advanced forms of communication are also typically part of an expedition's equipment. Today some expeditions have radios only at Base Camp; others use them at all camps up and down the mountain so that team members can warn each other of bad weather or call for help. The 1936 expedition was the first to use advanced communication technology, placing wireless telephone sets at each camp so that expedition members could communicate with one another as well as with the outside world. Today's expeditions sometimes include satellite phones and fax machines, making it possible for climbers and expedition leaders to communicate with the outside world instantaneously.

Climbing and Camping Gear

Even more important than communication equipment is the camping and climbing gear used on an expedition. Most of this gear is provided by expedition organizers, although a few pieces might be supplied by individual climbers. Most mountaineers, for example, own their own ice axe, one of the most vital tools of mountaineering in snow and ice.

At its most basic, an ice axe is a stick, or shaft, with a spike on one end and a steel head on the other. The head has a pick on one side and an adze (a scraping tool) on the other. The pick is usually curved or hooked to improve its ability to jab deep into snow and ice, and some picks have teeth for the same reason. The adze allows the climber to cut steps into hard snow and ice; it can be curved or flat, with straight or scalloped edges. The axe shaft was once made of wood, but today it is manufactured from aluminum, fiberglass, or a composite material, and it is sometimes covered at least partly by rubber for better grip. Its length can range from about sixteen inches to three feet, although in the past it could be as long as five feet.

Ice axes come in different weights and slightly different styles designed for different mixtures of rock, ice, and snow and for different angles of ascent. Therefore, many climbers carry more than one kind of ice axe. Basically, however, axes have three main purposes. First,

The Catapult

In trying to find a quick and effective way across one of Everest's most deadly crevasses, the sponsors of the 1953 expedition commissioned the invention of a catapult that would shoot a rope a great distance. One end of the rope would be fastened to the catapult; on the other end a hook called a grapnel would anchor the rope to the ice. The idea was that the mountaineer would use this taut, anchored rope to slide or inch across the divide. However, a demonstration of the catapult at one sponsor's estate proved disastrous. In his book *The Conquest of Everest*, expedition leader Sir John Hunt describes the demonstration.

"The gadget produced was extremely simple—two toggles for use as hand grips, at either end of a length of rubber rope, consisting of multiple strands of elastic. The grapnel was a wicked-looking affair, a kind of large wooden bullet armed with a number of hooked barbs. To this was attached a long nylon line. While watching the expert [demonstrating the device] laying out yard upon yard of this line, I expressed concern regarding the range of this weapon, for he had paid out some 150 yards, in contrast to the 80-yard length of the garden. Reassured on this point, Charles Wylie [another expedition member] and I took station at about a 6-foot interval, each holding a grip, while the demonstrator stretched the elastic behind us and attached to it the war head. Just when Charles and I were about to be pulled backwards off our feet, the missile was released. It shot high into the air with the nylon cord in its wake and was going very strongly over [the estate walls and toward the road], where it would most probably have speared a taxi or some unsuspecting pedestrian. Most fortunately, we were spared such a calamity by a tree, which intervened to arrest its flight some fifty feet up. On the whole, we thought, it was unlikely that . . . [Everest] would reserve for us any surprises meriting this kind of treatment."

Climbers on Mt. Everest typically use ropes to make their ascent or descent.

they act as canes that provide balance while climbing. Second, they can cut steps into the snow. Third, they are essential for performing an emergency maneuver known as the self-arrest, which involves jabbing the axe into the snow to stop, or arrest, a fall. American mountaineer Ed Webster describes his experience with a self-arrest:

> I tripped over a short icy step. A second later, I had the unpleasant realization that I was sliding down the mountain headfirst on my back. Instinctively, I clutched at my ice ax, jabbed the metal pick into the snow, pivoted my body uphill, jabbed my boots and crampon points [a series of metal spikes attached to the bottom of a boot] into the

snow—and stopped—all in several seconds. Trembling with fear, I ferociously kicked my crampon points into the hard ice buried beneath the top snow layer, and reestablished myself on the slope.[16]

Because falls like this are always a possibility, ropes are an important part of every Everest expedition. In an attempt to prevent falls, a stationary climber is often tied to a descending climber; the stationary climber gradually feeds out the rope using a device called a mechanical brake. If the descending climber starts to slip, the stationary climber applies the brake, thereby preventing the fall.

On commercial Everest expeditions, ropes are most commonly used to keep climbers on a

Clothing

It is important to wear the right clothing for mountaineering in snow and ice. Ideally, clothes should create an insulating air layer of warmth, fueled by body heat, against the skin. It is vital that this layer not be compromised by dampness. Prolonged moisture causes it to fail, and the result can be hypothermia—a deadly condition whereby the body experiences an uncontrolled drop in temperature from which it cannot recover. Hypothermia is one of the leading causes of death among climbers.

At the same time, mountaineers cannot afford to get too hot. Overheating leads to sweating, and sweating leads to dehydration. Since Everest's dry air also makes mountaineers dehydrated, overheating just compounds an already serious problem.

Mountaineers who will be exposed to snow and ice must wear the right clothing. Otherwise, they might get hypothermia, a condition whereby the body's temperature drops so low that the person could die. To help prevent mountaineers from getting too cold, clothes need to trap body heat against their skin. However, if a person gets too hot, the skin will sweat to reduce body temperature, a fact that can also result in hypothermia. Consequently, mountaineers layer their clothing to keep themselves warm and dry. The inner layer, right next to the skin, is made of polyester or polypropylene fabrics which draw moisture away from the body. The next layer, known as the insulating layer, is typically made of fleece, wool, or a wool/polyester blend and traps warm air next to the body. The final layer, called the shell, is usually made of nylon or synthetic fabrics that are lightweight yet water-proof and wind-resistant to keep water from getting in. Everest mountaineers select a nylon shell with two layers of fabric sewn together and filled with down, a natural material that offers great warmth. Down jackets are bulky and a bit cumbersome, but mountaineers welcome their protection against the elements.

preset path to the summit. Shortly after the first commercial expeditions began, Sherpas and expedition guides strung ropes along the best route to the peak. Today they continue to maintain these guide ropes, repairing or replacing those damaged by wind, snow, and rockslides. Mountaineers are clipped onto these guide ropes via a metal ring attached to a harness they wear. As the mountaineer walks, the ring slides freely along the guide rope. When an ascending climber meets a descending one, the former must unclip from the guide rope to allow the latter to pass, then clip his or her harness back on to the guide rope. In several places on the mountain, this system leads to traffic jams, where mountaineers trying to pass hold up a line of climbers behind them.

The composition of these mountaineering ropes has changed over the years. On the first Everest expeditions, climbers used ropes made of natural fibers. But during World War II nylon ropes were invented, and they have been used for mountaineering ever since. Although they are lightweight, nylon climbing ropes can bear more than two tons of weight. They are smooth, flexible, water-repellant, and come in a wide variety of sizes.

The same is true for tents and sleeping bags. Some tents are shaped like domes, others like tunnels. Some hold one person, some two, and others hold three, four, or five. Winter tents are heavy enough to withstand high winds and heavy snow; they generally have steep sidewalls to shed falling snow. Winter sleeping bags, like snow jackets, can be filled either with down or synthetic insulation.

Mountaineers must also take along a portable stove for cooking at high altitudes. Again, there are many choices in both the style of the stove itself and the fuel required to run it. Most mountaineering stoves weigh one to one and a half pounds, are sized to hold a quart-size pot, and will burn about a half pint of fuel an hour. The flame is generally directly under the pot and is fed fuel—usually butane—via a pressurized bottle.

Clothing

On some expeditions, stoves, tents, and sleeping bags are provided by organizers; on others, they are provided by the climbers themselves. When it comes to clothes, however, Western climbers almost always supply their own or wear outfits given to them by sponsors; meanwhile, Sherpas wear clothes provided to them by expedition organizers. Regardless, most people on Everest wear the same basic types of clothing.

In the early years of Everest expeditions, mountaineers used only natural-fiber clothes. For undergarments they relied on cotton, which today is known to be the worst fabric for climbing because it retains body moisture and loses warmth when wet. For outer garments, the early mountaineers wore heavy wool, layered for additional warmth. Eric Shipton describes his clothing on the day of his 1933 unsuccessful summit attempt:

> We donned every stitch of clothing we possessed. I wore a Shetland [wool] vest, a thick flannel shirt, a heavy camel-hair sweater, six light Shetland pullovers, two pairs of long Shetland pants, a pair of flannel trousers, and over all a silk-lined "Grenfell" windproof suit. A Shetland bal-

aclava [hat] and another helmet of "Grenfell" cloth protected my head, and my feet were encased in four pairs of Shetland socks and stockings. Gloves are always a problem on Everest, and the ideal glove that is warm yet flexible and will adhere to rocks has still to be designed; in this instance, a pair of woollen fingerless gloves inside a pair of South African lambskin gloves, also fingerless, kept my hands moderately warm.[17]

Modern climbers still use a layering system for their clothing, but unlike their predecessors, they have access to a wide variety of garments made from synthetic fibers that offer warmth without adding the weight or bulk of wool. In the coldest weather, mountaineers wear one- or two-piece down suits along with their customary down jackets. Hats are also a necessity, with string to tie them into place so wind will not carry them away. Gloves are essential to prevent frostbite. Most climbers wear heavy mittens with thin gloves underneath, taking the outer mittens off when they have to perform a task that requires manual dexterity.

Boots

Modern mountaineers also use a layered boot system that generally consists of liners, soft inner boots, hard-shell outer boots, and an overboot made of a synthetic rubber called neoprene. The latter is highly waterproof. Modern boots have benefited from technological advances that make them not only more waterproof than their predecessors but also more impervious to cold temperatures.

Before climbing in snow and ice, mountaineers strap on crampons, which are sets of metal spikes worn on the bottom of the boots. By jabbing these spikes into the snow and ice with each step, mountaineers can keep from slipping. There are a variety of crampons on the market, with different types and numbers of points and different ways of attaching to the boot.

Crampons were not used during the first Everest expeditions, even though they were available, because mountaineers believed that the crampons' tight straps would decrease blood circulation in the foot and encourage frostbite. Therefore, other means were used to make boots more stable. On the 1922 expedi-

tion, for example, mountaineers wore regular Alpine climbing boots with nails coming out of the soles to offer traction.

One of the most common complaints of mountaineers on early expeditions was that their boots did not fit properly. For instance, Hillary says of his 1953 expedition,

> None of us had particularly effective boots and the higher we went the more we suffered. . . . Winding in and out among the giant crevasses and great pinnacles of ice, we

Modern mountaineers wear neoprene boots and down-filled outer garments.

Climbers who test their equipment on shorter expeditions are usually better prepared for an intense Mt. Everest climb.

were always seeking a safe route while suffering agonies with our feet. . . . With cries of thankfulness [when we stopped to rest] we sat down, took off our boots and massaged our feet. It was at least an hour before we could continue with safety and comfort.[18]

Even modern climbers can have trouble with their boots, particularly if the boots are new. Mountaineers generally consider it vital to wear new boots several times before going on an expedition to soften them—or "break them in"—and make sure they will not hurt their feet. When Beck Weathers failed to do this before his 1996 expedition, he suffered for it on Everest:

I'd never bought the idea that you need to break in new mountaineering boots; either

they fit you from the beginning or they don't. . . . Unfortunately, the new boots rubbed both my shins, which soon were ulcerated [cut]. Wounds at high altitude do not heal. I knew I wouldn't recover until I was off the mountain. . . . [Consequently] each step was an agony. I had no choice, in the end, but to wrap my shins in bandages, suck it up and learn to live with it. There was no sense in complaining about something I couldn't change.[19]

Testing Equipment and Skills

Many mountaineers test not only their boots but also other types of gear before going to Everest. The 1953 expedition tested its mountaineering equipment by climbing Jungfraujoch (11,500

Color-Coded Tents

Some expeditions have used creative methods to organize their gear prior to embarking for Everest. The 1953 expedition, for instance, used different tents for different camps on the mountain, color-coding them to make it easier to choose the right tent for the right place. In his book *The Conquest of Everest*, Sir John Hunt explains that this expedition had about twenty tents

"of various shapes, sizes, and colors: three miniature ones intended for a final camp; orange ones for Advance Base and above; yellow ones of similar pattern to be used as far as the entrance to [a snowfield]; a distinctive Swiss tent which is Tenzing [Norgay's] temporary home, and two bigger dome-shaped tents, one used by the Sherpas and the other by ourselves. Beside some of them, pink, brown, and olive sleeping bags are spread out to air."

Some people believe that the success of the 1953 expedition was in part due to its high level of organization.

feet) in the Swiss Alps before heading to Everest, and they climbed up and down a 20,000-foot peak near Everest to recheck their equipment and help themselves get accustomed to high altitudes once in Nepal. Members of the 1963 expedition tried out their gear on Mt. Rainier (14,410 feet), and American mountaineer Woodrow Wilson Sayre prepared for his 1962 Everest climb by summitting 20,320-foot-high Mt. McKinley in Alaska.

Sayre needed to test his gear as well as his physical climbing skills because he knew little of the specialized mountaineering techniques for snow and ice. The first Sherpas to go on Everest expeditions also had to learn these skills. For example, Tenzing Norgay discusses his first expedition in 1935:

We were issued special clothes and boots and goggles. We ate strange foods out of tin cans. We used pressure stoves and sleeping bags and all sorts of other equipment I had never seen before. And in the actual climbing, too, there was much that I had to learn. Snow and glaciers themselves were nothing new to a boy who had grown up [at the base of Everest], but now for the first time I had experience with the real techniques of mountaineering: using a rope, cutting steps with an ax, making and breaking camps, choosing routes that are not only quick but safe.[20]

Just as expedition organizers are responsible for making preparations that benefit the expedition as a whole, so too must individual mountaineers be responsible for preparing themselves to meet the challenges of Everest. During the climb, one unprepared member can put the entire expedition in jeopardy. Therefore, even though having the right equipment in the right amount is essential, even the best equipment is worthless if the mountaineers do not know how to use it properly.

3 Individual Preparations

While organizers are outfitting the expedition, mountaineers must make their own individual preparations for the climb because those who do not adequately prepare themselves for Everest often do not get very far up the mountain. More than 60 percent of expeditions fail to get even a single member on the summit, and it is not unusual to encounter people on the lower slopes who have suddenly decided to abandon an expedition, pack up their gear, and go home. The most common reasons for giving up are illness, fatigue, intimidation, and the loss of motivation.

The latter is particularly common on commercial expeditions, where amateur climbers are often surprised at just how difficult an environment Everest really is. Experienced mountaineers often complain that these amateurs are neither physically nor mentally fit enough to be on Everest. For instance, American climber Ed Viesturs, who has summitted Everest, said while on the mountain in 1996, "A lot of people are up here who shouldn't be."[21]

Physical Training

To prepare for Everest, mountaineers are generally advised to follow a physical training program for several months prior to the expedition's start date. In most cases this training program involves exercises to increase muscle mass so they will be able to carry their oxygen tanks and personal camping equipment more easily up the mountain. Although Sherpas carry a lot of the expedition gear up the slopes, the typical load for mountaineers is still around forty pounds. On early expeditions some mountaineers routinely carried sixty pounds, the common weight load for a Sherpa today.

Another part of the physical training program for an Everest climb is some kind of exercise to improve overall fitness. The most popular exercises increase lung capacity and endurance, such as running. However, mountaineers must be careful not to hurt themselves during training. For example, amateur mountaineer Beck Weathers went on a daily run and lifted weights in preparation for his 1996 Everest expedition, but in doing so he damaged his muscles and joints. After he recovered, he hired an exercise expert, or personal trainer, to teach him how to exercise without reinjuring himself. Many mountaineers work with such trainers while preparing to climb Everest.

Weight Gain

Most mountaineers also follow an eating program designed to make them gain weight before their climb. They need extra fat reserves because most people lose thirty pounds during an Everest expedition. There are three main reasons for this weight loss. The first is that people often experience a lack of appetite at high altitudes. Mountaineer Eric Shipton says that this lack of appetite is

Mountaineers must be both physically and mentally prepared before undertaking a climb as daunting as one up Mt. Everest.

largely due to fatigue; he reports that on his 1933 Everest expedition the mountaineers

> tended to delude themselves that they had eaten a hearty meal. Over and over again I saw men starting for a long and exhausting day's work on the mountain with only a cup of cocoa and a biscuit or two inside them; the cold and wind discouraged eating during the climb, and they were generally too tired to eat anything much when they returned. This state of affairs contributed largely towards the rapid physical deterioration of the party.[22]

Another reason why climbers lose weight has to do with the labored breathing and dehydration that all mountaineers experience on Everest. While on a high-altitude climb, approximately 40 percent of a mountaineer's energy is expended just through breathing, and during this process the lungs can release as much as seven liters of water a day. Additional fluids are lost through sweating. Because of this water loss, the body becomes dehydrated, which in turn results in decreased weight. Even when fluids are replenished by drinking soup, water, tea, and other liquids, it is hard for a mountaineer to consume enough to recover the lost weight.

Altitude Sickness

Climbers must also prepare for physical dangers related to living at high altitude. To this end, mountaineers planning an Everest expedition typically teach themselves the symptoms of and treatments for altitude sickness, also known as acute mountain sickness (AMS). At its mildest, AMS can cause shortness of breath, coughing, fatigue, muscle weakness, insomnia, headache, nausea, vomiting, and/or loss of appetite. More serious cases of AMS can involve hypoxia, a condition in which the lower levels of oxygen during a climb affect the brain's ability to reason.

Hypoxia can make climbers confused enough to go off in the wrong direction or stop moving entirely. It can also make it difficult for the sufferer to choose the words to express him or herself. Perhaps the best description of this difficulty was provided by Shipton after his 1933 expedition:

I suddenly found that I could not articulate words properly. For example if I wished to say, "Give me a cup of tea," I would say something entirely different—maybe "tram-car, cat, put." It was a most aggravating situation. . . . I could not conceal it for long and I had to suffer the pitying looks of my

Climbers make camp at an altitude of 22,000 feet, where altitude sickness is not uncommon.

companions, who were obviously thinking, "Poor old Eric! Now he's gone bats." In actual fact I was perfectly clear-headed; I could even visualize the words I wanted to say, but my tongue just refused to perform the required movements.[23]

At its most severe, AMS can cause mountaineers to develop fluid in the lungs, a condition known as high-altitude pulmonary edema (HAPE). If the afflicted climbers do not go back down the mountain immediately, they will die—literally by drowning in their own fluids. A similar condition occurs when fluid develops in the brain, leaking from blood vessels into the skull. This condition is known as high-altitude cerebral edema (HACE). At first the symptoms are a deterioration of motor skills—which might mean that the climber can no longer walk, stand, or even crawl into a sleeping bag—and mental acuity to such an extent that hallucinations might occur. Eventually, if not treated, the brain's swelling will put the climber into a coma and result in death.

AMS affects people differently. Someone who has experienced AMS on one high-altitude climb should expect to experience it on another, although this is not always the case. Moreover, a high-altitude climber who has never gotten AMS before can still experience it on Everest. There is, therefore, no guarantee that a particular climber will not get AMS. However, the odds of getting the illness are greatly reduced when a mountaineer goes through a process known as acclimatization.

Acclimatization

With acclimatization, the mountaineer ascends the mountain gradually, allowing for rest periods at predetermined stages along the way. This gives the body a chance to adjust, or acclimate, to higher and higher elevations. Various changes occur in the human body during acclimatization. For instance, it gradually adjusts to functioning with less oxygen by producing more red blood cells, which carry oxygen throughout the body.

The speed with which a mountaineer can climb depends on the altitude. As Dr. Charles Houston explains,

Except for those who have had and fear they will again have mountain sickness, most people can go to 7,000 feet in one day from sea level and feel little discomfort. Above that—especially starting up a big mountain—2,000 feet of elevation gain a day is a reasonable rate, unless the effort is very strenuous. Above 17,000 feet, even this is too fast for some people. A demanding climb requires more oxygen for physical and mental effort, and both of these strain your resources. However, the better your acclimatization, the higher you can climb in a day.[24]

On extremely high mountains such as Everest, it is necessary to use a "one-step-forward, two-steps-backward" method to accomplish acclimatization, with the mountaineer going up in altitude, then back down again, then up a little farther than before, then back down again. This up-and-down process continues throughout the climb. Some people react well to this process, feeling fit at high altitudes within a relatively short time. Others, though, require much longer to feel well while on Everest.

Rather than spend weeks acclimatizing on Everest, mountaineers who can afford the expense go to Switzerland or some other high country prior to embarking for Everest to begin the acclimatization process in advance of the expedition. Alternatively, some people arrive early in Nepal or Tibet to adjust to the altitude

As climbers ascend Mt. Everest, they must use a "one-step-forward, two-steps-backward method" of accomplishing acclimatization.

there and climb a few of the smaller Himalayan peaks before tackling Everest. Other people try to avoid taking the time to acclimatize by instead taking a pill called Diamox (which is the medication acetazolamide) once they start ascending the mountain. This medicine makes the climber breathe more often and more deeply, thereby drawing more oxygen into the body. However, the pill's manufacturers are unwilling to call it a preventative because, so far, it

has only been scientifically tested for treating the symptoms of altitude sickness after they begin to occur.

Combatting AMS

Some mountaineers prepare themselves for AMS by acquiring an emergency injection kit containing a syringe filled with a dose of the drug dexamethasone, which counteracts the effects of HACE or HAPE. In many cases, one shot of dexamethasone will provide climbers with approximately six to twelve hours of relief from symptoms, enough to allow them the physical and mental ability to descend to a safer altitude. However, it is still important to get climbers afflicted with AMS off the mountain as quickly as possible because death can occur within six to twelve hours.

This time frame can be extended by administering oxygen and/or placing the victim in a Gamow bag, a portable chamber that simulates low-altitude conditions. Invented by Dr. Igor Gamow, this device is simple to use. A climber suffering from altitude sickness is placed inside the bag, which is made of orange nylon, and other climbers use a foot pump to fill it with air. This not only provides the sick climber with oxygen but also increases air pressure in the bag to approximate conditions at lower altitudes.

Because the correct use of the Gamow bag can mean the difference between life and death, many mountaineers practice with the bag before they embark on an expedition. Danish mountaineer Lene Gammelgaard describes her own practice session with a Gamow bag:

> Because Dale [a climber in her group] is tall, we pick him to play "victim" as we practice using the Gamow bag. It's quite a hassle, stuffing a "semiconscious" guy into the cigar-shaped bag, but finally a smiling Dale peeps up through the little plastic window. The oxygen saturation in Dale's blood increases from 75 percent to 98 percent within very few pumps; simultaneously, his pulse decreases. Martin [another climber in the group], the appointed pump-man, might soon need an oxygen refill himself after his contribution—it's hard work maintaining a constant, sufficient pressure inside the bag at this altitude.[25]

Health Concerns

Because of the physical risks involved with climbing Everest, some mountaineers take courses in emergency high-altitude medicine before embarking on an expedition. Others become obsessed with thinking about all of the things that could go wrong with their health. At least one mountaineer, Raymond Lambert of the 1952 Swiss expedition, had his appendix surgically removed before his expedition for fear that he would develop appendicitis while on Everest. He often recommended that others do the same.

Although most mountaineers do not go to such extremes, almost all of them do have a physical checkup before leaving on their expedition. All travelers to Nepal and Tibet must be inoculated against four diseases common in the Himalayan region: tetanus, hepatitis B, meningococcal meningitis, and typhoid. All travelers must also have a visa to enter Nepal or Tibet. Without this official document, a mountaineer cannot enter either of these countries; travelers have to show the visa to government officials at the border or, if traveling by plane, at the airport. Any airplane passengers who arrive in Nepal without a visa are required to fill out the necessary papers and wait at the airport until a visa is issued to them.

Mountaineers also typically have a dental exam before embarking for Nepal because extreme cold and high altitude can cause fillings to crack and/or fall out. Eye exams are critical as well because evidence suggests that an eye disease called glaucoma can worsen on Everest, and officials warn that anyone diagnosed with this disease should probably not go on the expedition.

The eyes experience many stresses while on Everest. For example, the air on the mountain is so dry it can make contact lenses painful to wear. In addition, the changes in air pressure

Since a communicable disease could wipe out an entire expedition, Western mountaineers routinely get themselves vaccinated for serious illnesses prior to leaving for Asia, and anyone showing signs of such a disease must leave the expedition immediately. Sometimes, however, the signs of illness are not readily apparent. In his book *Americans on Everest*, James Ramsey Ullman reports on a problem encountered by his 1963 expedition.

"[En route to Base Camp] . . . several of the expedition members had noticed that one of the younger low-level porters, a Sherpa boy of thirteen or so, was behaving in strange fashion: moving very slowly along the trail minus a load and with his face almost hidden by a burlap rag. And when they stopped to investigate they found that his face was grossly swollen and covered with pustules. . . . [The expedition doctors] were summoned. Like most American doctors, they had had no direct experience with smallpox [because the disease has been all but eradicated in the United States]. But they knew it when they saw it—and here it was. The boy had been with the baggage train all the way from Kathmandu. For the past three days, it was discovered, his condition had been known to many of the other porters, who had shunned him both on the trail and at the nightly campsites. But no one had reported it to any member of the expedition. Now, of course, he was immediately detached from the party. Under the doctors' supervision, he was put in isolation in a nearby village and given such makeshift treatment as was possible. But he had reached the stage where, in effect, nothing could be done for him, and a few days [later] . . . word reached the expedition that he had died. Team members and high-climbing Sherpas had all been recently vaccinated—the former at home, the latter in Kathmandu. But the other Sherpas . . . had no such protection, and how many had been infected (smallpox has a ten- to twelve-day incubation period) no one knew."

that occur as climbers reach high altitudes can cause the eyes to change shape somewhat, particularly in people who have scar tissue from eye surgeries used to improve vision. This can cause temporary blindness in some individuals. For instance, Beck Weathers, who had eye surgery before his 1996 Everest expedition, became temporarily blind while near the summit and could not make it down the mountain unaided. Sometimes such blindness is preceded by other visual problems. During the 1924 expedition, climber Edward Norton experienced double vision once he was above 27,000 feet, and, after he had descended a few thousand feet, he experienced temporary blindness for more than sixty hours.

Mountaineers can also become temporarily blind if they stare at the snow for long periods. Houston explains:

[Snow blindness] is a painful form of *conjunctivitis* (inflammation of the outer "skin-like" covering of the eyeball) due to too much ultraviolet light. Most often it happens when a person doesn't wear appropriate protective glasses on a bright sunny day while on snow, but it is a real risk in fog or under thin clouds, which allow UV light to be reflected off the snow. And UV light is more intense the higher you go. I can't stress too strongly the importance of good sunglasses, with side shields, on a high

Climbers wear protective goggles at high altitudes to prevent snow blindness.

snowy mountain or indeed on any snow-covered landscape.[26]

At extremely high altitudes without protective glasses, the retinas of the eyes burn from the intense sun, and within ten minutes the mountaineer will be blind. As a result, climbers always bring good goggles with them to Everest; some even bring two pairs in case of accident or damage because without eye protection they would have to abandon their quest for the summit. Since skin can burn too, climbers also bring along a substance called glacier cream to coat their ears and nose as protection against ultraviolet rays.

Mental Preparations

All of these physical preparations can reduce the odds that a mountaineer will have problems on Everest, but, of course, the risks on the mountain are still great. Sometimes an awareness of these risks can cause a mountaineer to lose confidence in the climb and consider canceling the trip. Consequently, one of the most important preparations a person can make before climbing Everest is to develop a positive attitude. About her own attempts to do this, Gammelgaard says,

I shut out—consciously—all doubts, all thoughts of death, frostbite and turning around because of bad storms. And I make myself alarmingly goal-oriented, narrow-minded. . . . Selectively, I study the accounts of successful expeditions and communicate with people who have a playful, positive attitude toward mountaineering. My incentive is to code my mind with enough positive input to overrule my own healthy scepticism and to forget the stories I myself have gathered over the years as arguments against climbing mountains.[27]

Many people believe that if a mountaineer does not have the right mental attitude during a climb, physical preparations will mean little in terms of whether that mountaineer will make it to the top of Everest. As Weathers explains, "Your body doesn't carry you up there. Your mind does. Your body is exhausted hours before you reach the top; it is only through will and focus and drive that you continue to move. If you lose that focus, your body is a dead, worthless thing beneath you."[28]

To prepare for the mental stresses of climbing Everest, some mountaineers learn meditation techniques, believing they will help them stay calm and focused on the mountain. Others engage in hard physical activities that push their minds and bodies to the limit of their endurance, believing that by meeting and overcoming these challenges they will be better able to meet and overcome the challenges of Everest.

But even though mountaineers planning their first Everest climb would like to think otherwise, no amount of preparation can truly ensure that someone will be able to endure the mental stresses they will experience on the mountain. Everest has a way of either breaking or strengthening the will of those who ascend its slopes. As adventure filmmaker Matt Dickinson, who summitted Everest from the north side in 1996, explains,

Mountains peel layers away from a climber like a scrapper dismantles a car at a junk yard. They strip off veneers and shells, leaving just the distilled essence of a person behind, the chassis on which the body panels are bolted. Seemingly placid [expedition] group members might burst into sudden, violent, rages. Hard-talking . . . men might be reduced to tears. Mousey matrons might become mountain lions, thundering up peaks and down valleysides at superhuman speeds.[29]

Because climbers often change in temperament while on Everest, it is hard to tell who will make it to the top and who will not. According to Henry Todd, who runs a commercial expedition company and has helped many people reach Everest's summit,

Just Too Dangerous

As people begin to prepare themselves mentally for their climb, some decide that an Everest expedition is too dangerous for parents. For example, in reading mountaineering books prior to her departure for Everest, Lene Gammelgaard concluded that she would have to summit before she had any children—an opinion she maintained after her climb was over. In her book *Climbing High,* she explains her opinion.

"I cannot respect men who have kids and simultaneously participate in this deadly game. . . . I imagine that when I choose to have children, I will give up my participation in the race to summit the fourteen 8,000-meter peaks. The way I see it now, it's an either/or situation because the risk of dying while climbing is so huge. Just study a few expedition accounts to calculate the odds—they are bad!"

Sheer will and the strength of mind and body are essential for a successful Everest summit.

You can [have] the best climbers [that is, the most physically fit] not perform, and you can get other people who are very marginal who are just utterly determined and will be successful. I've had this happen to me again and again. I've taken someone whom I thought, if anyone fails, it will be him, and he's just waltzed up. And someone whom I've taken thinking, "Hey, here's a 'cert' [someone certain to succeed], put a tick by his name before we go," and he hasn't done it.[30]

No one knows what will happen on the mountain. "Expect the unexpected" is common advice for mountaineers ascending any high peak. But while no amount of preparation can guarantee success, going to Everest unprepared is folly. Both the mind and body must be ready for the challenge of the climb. As mountaineer James Ramsey Ullman says, "An attempt on Everest is no less a thing of the spirit than of lung and limb. What a mountaineer brings with him in his mind and heart is as essential as what he brings in the pack on his back."[31]

From Katmandu to Base Camp

The first expeditions left for Everest from Darjeeling, India, traveling through Tibet via old trading routes. Today, however, mountaineers typically begin their expedition in the city of Katmandu (also spelled Kathmandu) in Nepal, which has the closest major airport to Everest. Katmandu is also the place where most expeditions hire their porters and Sherpas, either just before leaving Katmandu for Everest or during an advance trip to Nepal.

Expeditions can also buy last-minute supplies in Katmandu. Most expeditions purchase their gear in advance, then send it to the city by air or, prior to the airport's establishment, by ship or train. Nonetheless, it is not uncommon for a mountaineer to replace a broken, lost, or forgotten item after landing in Nepal. The primary place to shop for such items is Tamel, the city's tourist market area. Mountaineer Matt Dickinson calls Tamel "one of the joys of Kathmandu" and speaks approvingly of "the wood-carved interiors of Tamel cafes, [where] chocolate cake and banana fritters are served."[32]

But Katmandu also has its negative aspects. Noisy, dirty, and filled with foul odors, it is a chaotic city with heavy automobile traffic and seemingly no traffic laws. Although there are many modern buildings, there are also cows and water buffalo defecating in the streets. Human waste soils many areas too.

The filth of Katmandu can make people sick. Airborne particles from its waste can cause respiratory illnesses and contaminate water sources; bacteria from feces can find their way into food at restaurants and markets. Eating this food can give climbers severe diarrhea before they reach Everest. Therefore, most climbers are eager to leave Katmandu for the slopes of Everest.

Main temple in Katmandu, the city where expedition members normally stop to hire their guides.

Rising Altitude

The expedition members, guides, porters, and Sherpas typically travel as a group from Katmandu to the mountain. Their route is different depending on whether they plan to ascend the north or the south side of Everest. In either case, the trail leads the expedition to increasingly higher altitudes. Katmandu is located 4,344 feet above sea level; Base Camp on the north side of Everest is at approximately 18,000 feet and on the south at 17,600 feet.

A mountaineer must allow roughly ten to twelve days to make the ascent to either of these camps to adjust properly to the changes in altitude. Moreover, physicians recommend that people go no higher than ninety-five hundred feet before resting for several days to begin the acclimation process. Furthermore, as mountaineers travel higher, they continue to stop along the way to give their bodies time to adjust to altitude increases because, according to Weathers, "Your body simply cannot withstand the enormous physiologic shock of being suddenly placed in such an oxygen-deprived environment [that is, a high altitude with low oxygen levels]."[33]

During the acclimation process, the body begins using oxygen more efficiently. Respiratory and heart rates increase, and the bone marrow produces more than the usual number of oxygen-carrying red blood cells. Body tissues also change in order to withstand lower air pressure. This means that, with time, mountaineers can go higher without feeling ill effects. Moreover, mountaineers who take their time getting to Base Camp generally feel better when they reach the mountain. Nonetheless, some people rush their journey, too eager to get to Everest to worry about the consequences.

The Southern Trek

But even eager mountaineers find it hard to move quickly on the southern route to the mountain. The 180-mile trail from Katmandu to Base Camp is inaccessible by automobiles, so

Leeches

Many trekkers to Base Camp on the south have complained about leeches. Sir Edmund Hillary was one, and Earl Denman—who attempted a solo ascent without a permit in 1947—was another. In his book *Alone to Everest*, Denman writes about his encounters with these blood-sucking worms.

"It rained lightly as we passed along the verge of a wood. The conditions were ideal for leeches, which we had not encountered so far, and there were many of them in evidence. I had read a great deal about the loathsome habits of these creatures, and all the worst that I had read proved true. They are small worms . . . [with] two suckers, one at each end, and they move by looping like a caterpillar. . . . Their jaws can be moved independently . . . and once they have gained a hold they are difficult to remove, until they fall away of their own accord when sated with blood. . . . It is said that the most effective ways of removing them are by applying a lighted cigarette, or salt, for which they have a natural aversion. . . . Although I carried small bags of salt, with strings to attach them to the wrists, I found it better on this occasion to keep a sharp eye out for them and remove them before they had gained a hold on the flesh."

mountaineers must walk—or in mountaineering terms, trek—in the heat, high humidity, and dust, up and down steep hills and through valleys and forests. Part of the trail is paved with stones provided by nearby villagers, but other sections are muddy or rutted.

During the first few days of this trek, much of the mountaineers' time is usually spent walking behind pack-laden animals. The line of men and animals can be quite formidable on large expeditions, sometimes stretching five miles or more. Many mountaineers have likened it to an army on the march, an appropriate comparison given that many of the early expeditions were led by British military men.

When the animals can go no farther on the difficult road, porters take over their loads. Tenzing Norgay explains why:

> At the bottom of every valley was a river, and no horse or mule could manage the hanging and swaying plank bridges that are the only way across them. . . . This is one of the reasons why, through all the centuries, the Nepalese have carried their loads on their own backs. And even today any travelers through the country must do the same.[34]

Today crowds of tourists are a big problem on the southern trek. In 1996 approximately four hundred thousand tourists traveled to the Base Camp on south Everest, although only a few hundred planned to climb to the mountain's summit. Sometimes there are so many people on the route that the path becomes clogged and slow-moving.

There are several villages along the trail, the largest of which is Namche Bazar. Considered the capital of the Sherpa lands, it is noted for its experienced Sherpa climbers. In fact, their reputation is so excellent that some expedition organizers wait until they reach Namche Bazar to hire their staff's top Sherpas.

Namche Bazar is considered the Sherpa capital and a good place to rest before beginning an Everest climb.

Namche Bazar is located at 9,000 feet, which is around the point where physicians recommend that mountaineers rest to begin their acclimation process. Therefore, most expeditions spend a few days there before moving on. In recent years, however, some amateur mountaineers have chosen instead to bypass Namche Bazar, taking a helicopter from a much lower altitude directly to a point above 16,000 feet. Since the Base Camp on the south side of Everest is at

17,600 feet, this helicopter shortcut saves a great deal of time. However, it almost guarantees that the mountaineer will suffer at least a mild form of altitude sickness, with severe headaches and nausea. But again, some mountaineers are so eager to get to Everest that they do not heed advice to travel slowly.

The Northern Route

On the north, mountaineers do not make the long journey from Katmandu to Everest on foot. The road there is accessible by vehicles, and the Chinese government—which rules Tibet—insists that every expedition drive rather than walk. Mountaineers typically arrive at the town of Tatopani, on the border of Nepal and Tibet, after driving eight hours from Katmandu in hired cars. There, they cross a bridge that links Nepal with the Chinese-controlled territory, and once on the other side they are met by representatives of the Tibetan Mountaineers' Association (TMA), also controlled by the Chinese government. TMA representatives handle all transportation from this point on and set the pace at which the expedition proceeds. Only after all of the mountaineers' supplies have been transferred to official TMA vehicles, driven by TMA drivers, can the group begin the journey to Everest.

The drive from the border to the north Base Camp can be made in one day. However, such a rapid increase in altitude would make the mountaineers feel sick when they got there. Consequently, TMA representatives arrange for them to stay overnight in a few villages along the way, leaving them at government-approved hotels. Westerners are usually surprised by the bleakness of these accommodations. Matt Dickinson describes his hotel in Zangmu, a town on the northern route to Everest:

The hotel was a cold, eerie place, with echoing corridors and missing windows through which the evening rain clouds drifted. Flooded spittoons and overflowing ashtrays lurked in the stairwells. The rooms were filled with an odd assortment of Day-Glo green and orange nylon furniture. . . . The restaurant was in the basement, next to a deserted bar that was barricaded by a padlock and chain. We sat in a depressed huddle around a circular table, eating green vegetables and rice with pork, washed down with beer that was so flat it contained not a single bubble of gas.[35]

From Zangmu, the route winds through forests and mountains scarred by rockslides. Sometimes the road becomes so narrow that it appears the vehicles are going to tip over the side of the mountain. Eventually, though, they reach the Rongbuk Valley and the Tibetan Base Camp, located at approximately eighteen thousand feet at the base of Everest's north face. The entire journey from Katmandu to this location generally takes ten days. The mountaineers then rest at Base Camp for several weeks before making their first ascent up Everest.

Base Camp

It takes roughly ten weeks of living at either the north or the south Base Camp for a mountaineer to adjust fully to the altitude. Additional time is sometimes spent waiting for the weather to clear. Therefore, during much of the climbing season both camps are filled with mountaineers, guides, Sherpas, cooks, medical personnel, and workers from several expeditions.

Roughly three hundred support personnel stay in the south Base Camp during the climbing season, with another two hundred Sherpas and mountaineers waiting to summit. About

On the trail to Base Camp on the south side of Everest, mountaineers encounter many rivers. In his book *View from the Summit*, Sir Edmund Hillary describes one such encounter during his 1953 Everest expedition, during which he helped not only his own porters but also thirty locals across the water.

"We came to a mighty stream, 200 yards across and sweeping down with great vigor. Thirty local porters with their own extremely heavy loads on the way to market were squatting together beside the bank obviously too afraid to cross. But we were not prepared to wait for the river to go down.... [A teammate] and I ... moved into the water.... Wave after wave swept past us, the water was up to our waists as we shuffled slowly across.... It was an exhilarating experience and we were laughing with pleasure as we emerged on the far bank. Nearby was a cluster of young trees and with my ice axe I hacked out a bough about eight feet long. We held the long pole in the line of the speeding water and helped by its extra weight and support we made an easier return trip to our Sherpas and porters. Then with five or six laden porters clinging to the tree trunk we crossed the wide stream with ease. Backward and forward we went ... [until we had helped everyone across]."

two hundred mountaineers and two hundred support personnel stay at the north Base Camp during this time. Many mountaineers find the north Base Camp bleaker than the south one. This is partly because the climate and the terrain on the north side of Everest's base is harsher. As Dickinson, who stayed in the north Base Camp in 1996, reports,

A more hostile, less heartening, spot would be hard to imagine.... Arriving expeditions scatter themselves far and wide across the glacial valley, seeking out shallow dips and hollows that they imagine will protect them from the wind. They are wrong. The wind of Tibet is inescapable—it is part of the fabric of the place, like the stones and the dust. And the smell of stale yak [excrement]....

Every tiny feature of the Rongbuk Valley conspires to make life more difficult. The ground is frozen, and cannot be penetrated by even the sturdiest tent peg. The rivers are frozen too, or where they run they are filled with silt and cannot be drunk. Sleeping bags, put out to air, are picked up by the wind and whipped away. Washed clothes freeze as stiff as boards. The air is dry, adding to the draining effects of altitude. Throats become sore. Lips become cracked. Fingers split and get infected. Minds start to wander, thinking of home—thinking of anything but the terrifying mountain that sits above the valley.[36]

Everything at the north Base Camp is brought there by expedition members each year. Each expedition establishes its own campsite within Base Camp and pitches its tents apart from other expeditions. Since strong winds make it difficult to remain outside for very long, people generally stick to their own campsites and remain in their tents most of the time.

Permanent Structures

In contrast, the south Base Camp is like a small city. Each expedition pitches its tents apart

Generally, several different expeditions camp together and use a common tent for cooking or dining.

from the others, but the campsite also has cook tents and dining tents where people from more than one expedition can mingle. These are permanent structures with stone walls and tarpaulin roofs. Solid roofs are not used because the south Base Camp sits on a glacial ice flow that is continually moving, and the roofs would collapse on people as the ground shifts. For the same reason, the stone walls must be repaired each spring; teams of Sherpas work together to prepare the buildings before the climbing season begins.

An expedition might also hire Sherpas to provide it with a latrine made of stone, with an opening in the back where waste can be removed using a shovel. Lene Gammelgaard describes one such structure:

The crowning achievement of our camp is a stunning [latrine] . . . in stone, with high walls on the three sides. . . . The fourth half-wall faces [Mount] Pumori, so you can enjoy a view of that peak and the nearby glacier lakes. The sky serves as roof, and the tarpaulin door is fixed to an odd arrangement of strings, so that your dignity is safe even in a stiff gale. The floor is laid with big, flat tiles of rock leaving an opening over a deep . . . hole like an old-fashioned privy. All your business must be done while standing, though. At first, the hole was too wide—one misstep and you'd vanish down the hole into the growing pile of [waste]. The construction was improved with splendid results, but they had to raise the floor, so now the upper part of your body sticks up in the open.[37]

There is a great deal of refuse scattered all around the perimeter of both camps, including not only toilet paper and waste—which, because of the cold, doesn't degrade—but also empty oxygen canisters. This debris has been piling up for years, and because the ground is essentially barren at this altitude, none of it is hidden from view. Prompted by environmentalists, Nepal recently established a rule that all expeditions had to remove their own trash; Tibet, however, has no such rule.

Disparities in Equipment

Although some structures in the south Base Camp are permanent, most are temporary tents provided by each expedition. Prior to the climbing season, advance teams of Sherpas and other expedition employees stake out each expedition's site at Base Camp and pitch enough tents to claim their spot. Staking a claim is necessary because more than a dozen expeditions now compete for space on each side of Everest every year.

Living conditions among the expeditions vary. In 1996, for example, most expeditions had only the most basic necessities, with mountaineers sleeping together in four- or five-person tents. Two expensive commercial expeditions, however, had private tents, a portable shower, advanced communication equipment, and many other luxuries not usually associated with camping in difficult terrain.

Continuing the Acclimatization Process

Despite modern amenities, the first few days in Base Camp are unpleasant because people are not yet acclimated to its altitude. This results in labored breathing and fatigue. As Beck Weathers says, "When you first arrive at Base Camp, you are acutely aware that every motion you make seems to suck the oxygen out of your body."[38] Many people also experience headaches and nausea. As time passes, however, breathing eases and feelings of illness disappear. When this happens, mountaineers are ready to make brief forays higher and higher up the mountain, with long rests in between. Each time they climb, though, their physical discomfort returns until their bodies have adapted to each new level of altitude.

Acclimation plans vary depending on what expedition leaders believe is best for their mountaineers. One common approach, though, is to have mountaineers make four acclimatization excursions, each time to a higher point on the mountain. After the first climb they descend to Base Camp to rest, but after the other three excursions they sleep at a successively higher camp on the mountain for a night before descending to Base Camp to rest.

By sleeping at a higher altitude for a night, mountaineers adapt more quickly to Everest's upper altitudes. However, the human body can comfortably adjust only to an altitude of 19,685 feet. Beyond that, acclimatization becomes increasingly difficult, and by 22,965 feet no one can make such an adjustment; the body's cells deteriorate, and various organs gradually fail. Above 24,606 feet the rate of this failure is so fast that climbers cannot afford to linger in the region very long. In fact, no one can live more than five days at this altitude without descending, even with supplemental oxygen.

Throughout the acclimation process, mountaineers must look for the warning signs of altitude sickness and move down the mountain quickly if they notice any of them. Consequently, experienced guides like Anatoli Boukreev warn mountaineers that even when they are following an acclimation plan they must proceed at their own pace:

> We reminded . . . [the climbers] that they needed to carefully monitor the condition of their bodies, being constantly aware that at high altitude their sensations and reactions would not be altogether familiar. We could do our jobs as guides and monitor them, but only they would know the interior truth [about whether they were feeling ill]. . . . We reinforced the importance of always maintaining a reserve, not allowing yourself to get totally depleted, being careful to understand that "I can't" usually means exactly that. You can't and you shouldn't. Stop, turn around, and save your life.[39]

Ultimately, it is the individual mountaineer who is responsible for monitoring his or her own health, and most take this responsibility seriously. In his book *The Climb*, Boukreev quotes one mountaineer as saying, "People become totally self-absorbed, monitoring their bodies, whether they're peeing or not, what their urine looks like, whether they're pooping every day, whether they're nauseous, whether they have a headache or not."[40]

Boredom

Besides worrying about health, there is little to do at Base Camp. It is a place to rest the body, but in the process the mind often becomes bored. Many people cope with this situation by reading. However, because books are heavy, mountaineers try not to carry too many to Base Camp, and when not reading, they have a lot of time to think. This can lead to doubts regarding their mountaineering skills and their desire to climb Everest.

To prevent their clients from dwelling on negative thoughts, commercial expeditions in the south Base Camp often organize entertaining group activities. These include parties, games, and contests. Commercial expeditions also encourage their clients to eat together. Many climbers, though, prefer to eat when they feel like it, and some kind of food is always available in the dining tent.

The mountaineers themselves also develop creative methods to stay entertained. For example, Weathers says,

> The major rigor of Base Camp is boredom; you spend a lot of time getting ready to do things, and a lot of time recovering from doing them, and therefore a lot of time do-

A Leisurely Routine

In his book *The Conquest of Everest*, Sir John Hunt describes the daily routine on the 1953 expedition's trek to Base Camp.

"We followed a leisurely routine. We would rise at 5:30 A.M. with the aid of a cup of tea. The whole caravan would be on the move soon after 6 A.M. Our kitchen staff would go ahead . . . to select a suitable place for breakfast. . . . Ar-

riving at some delectable stream after two to three hours, we would make a prolonged halt, and while the cook made his fire and prepared porridge, eggs and bacon, we would swim and rest, some reading or writing, others watching birds, catching butterflies and insects. Camp would be reached in the early afternoon, allowing plenty of time to settle in, write diaries and dispatches, and discuss future plans."

At a Base Camp, climbers often eat together and socialize in an effort to relieve boredom.

ing nothing. . . . I brought along . . . [a book], to help beguile the hours, plus a little book on learning to juggle, a skill I thought would be fun to master. I became a familiar camp figure, fumbling away in front of my tent. Those of us who had trouble keeping the Sherpas' names straight also used the downtime to take Polaroids [instant photographs] of them and then memorize their faces.[41]

Prayer Wheels

Prior to and after an Everest expedition, some Westerners and Sherpas spin a special prayer wheel and say prayers to offer respect to the gods and to honor those who have died on the mountain. In his book *Tiger of the Snows*, Tenzing Norgay tells of one prayer wheel in his own native village.

"For important occasions, as well as for whoever would use it, we have in [the village of] Toong Soong Busti a small temple. And inside it is only one thing: a great prayer wheel, almost twice the height of a man, that almost fills the single room. A rope is attached to it, so that it may be set spinning, and when it spins it rings a gong. Often when you pass the temple you can hear it, sounding for a birth or a death, or simply because someone is there praying. . . . It is sounding not only for the newborn or the dead, but for all of us who are turning slowly on the Wheel of Life."

Although some people at the south Base Camp remain in their tents, others find it enjoyable to sit outside together and talk, providing it is not windy. It can be surprisingly warm on the mountain. Because of the thin air, under a clear sky the sun beats down very strongly, and even with snow on the ground the spring temperature is sometimes one hundred degrees Fahrenheit at midday. Other times, though, the weather can be particularly brutal. In 1963, for instance, it was so cold that an expedition physician wrote, "Most of the time everything in the place, including me, is frozen solid and must be thawed before use—even my ballpoint pen, which I have to hold over a candle after writing each sentence."[42]

Appeasing the Gods

Because Base Camp is so boring, people are eager to leave it for their first ascent. Before this happens, however, the Sherpas perform a climbing ceremony called a *puja*. The preparations for the *puja* begin in Katmandu, where the expedition members purchase prayer flags. Once on the mountain, Sherpas build a stone cairn, or memorial, consisting of piled stones, just over six feet tall right outside the camp and display the flags there. On the day of the ceremony, which usually occurs the night before the first climb, the expedition's food and climbing gear are placed against the cairn, where a holy man blesses them. If anything goes wrong during this ceremony, it is considered a bad omen. For example, on one occasion the central flagpole of the cairn broke shortly after it was put into place, and the Sherpas were afraid to climb the mountain.

Gammelgaard describes a *puja* conducted on the south side of Everest in 1996:

[On the prescribed day] haze and fragrance from the lit incense hang above the altar. . . . Three Sherpas recite from the oblong scripture books. Though I don't understand the actual words, I nonetheless come under the spell of the solemn ambience. The rice-throwing ritual is about to begin. Rice is distributed, and when the Sherpas throw it into the air, we follow their example. . . . Most important now is tying the lama-blessed red bands around our necks. They will protect us against all evil and bring us back safely from our risky journey. . . . All [of our ice] axes are on the altar, being blessed, and will remain in the care of the Gods overnight.

First thing in the morning, before dawn's break, we'll pick them up on our way to [ascend the mountain].[43]

The Tibetans and Nepalese have long believed Everest to be holy, and this ceremony is meant to appease the gods of the mountain so they will not harm the mountaineers. The Tibetans call Everest Chomolungma, translated as "the Goddess Mother of the World" or "the Goddess Mother of the Wind." The Nepalese call it Sagarmatha, or "the Goddess of the Sky." Sherpas never fail to ask for the gods' permission before climbing, and out of either superstition or religious belief, many Western mountaineers do the same.

Only after performing the *puja* are the Sherpas willing to climb, and without the

Expedition members take part in a climbing ceremony called a puja.

Sherpas no expedition can be assured of success. Even when Sherpas are not needed to help the mountaineers themselves, they typically go ahead of the mountaineers to establish the route and campsites. They are also always eager to ascend the mountain to rescue stranded mountaineers.

Because Sherpas live in the Himalayas, they do not have to follow the acclimation process of other mountaineers. They are ready to climb whenever the expedition members are willing and able to depart from Base Camp. This occurs once the expedition leader has decided that the weather is right and that all of his or her mountaineers are in good enough physical shape—with no obvious symptoms of altitude sickness—to make the first foray upward.

Climbing the Lower Slopes

Once acclimated to Base Camp, mountaineers begin climbing to camps higher and higher on the mountain and going back down to Base Camp between climbs. Sherpas establish these camps by pitching tents at each site prior to the mountaineers' first ascent. For many years the location of the camps differed annually, but over time certain spots became the traditional campsites for every climbing season.

Each camp is designated with a roman numeral—Camp I, Camp II, Camp III, and so on—with larger numbers being closer to the summit. On the north side, however, the first camp up Everest's slopes is called Advanced Base Camp, with Camp I coming after that. The reason for this is that once mountaineers have become fully acclimated to the altitude of the north base camp, they relocate their supplies higher up on the mountain, using Advanced Base Camp as their starting point for climbs for the rest of their time on the mountain.

Ascending to Advanced Base Camp

The ascent to Advanced Base Camp is more of a hike than a climb because the route is not particularly steep. Even supply-laden animals can make the eighteen-mile journey in only three days. However, the path has many rocks and ice patches that can sometimes make walking difficult. As one climber described it, "The path was inconsistent, sometimes rising, sometimes falling,

and defying any attempt to get [our walking] into a rhythm. Splashes of red blood marked the snow at regular intervals, for many of the yaks had cut their feet on the sharp terrain."[44]

The route goes over frozen rivers and past frozen lakes and freestanding ice towers called seracs. Everest has many seracs, at heights ranging from a few feet to one hundred feet tall. They are highly unstable because ice melting within the structure can suddenly cause a piece to break off. In fact, the warmer weather that occurs on Everest in the spring can transform many aspects of the mountain's icy terrain through melting. For instance, ice ponds can gradually disappear, leaving craters in the ground.

At Advanced Base Camp, which lies at around eighteen thousand feet, there are numerous patches of ice and snow along with many hard rocks. This rocky terrain makes tent floors uncomfortable. Nonetheless, mountaineers remain in their tents most of the time because there is little to see or do. The area has no foliage; it is very bleak. As mountaineer Matt Dickinson explains, Advanced Base Camp

> makes Base Camp seem like a Caribbean resort. Squeezed into a narrow rocky strip of rubble between the dirty ice of . . . [a] glacier and the decaying rock wall of . . . [a neighboring mountain], it is not a location in which relaxation comes easily. The terrain is unrelentingly brutal; walking from one tent to another is an obstacle course of lurking crevasses and ankle-twisting rocks.[45]

The Ice Wall

As in Base Camp, mountaineers in Advanced Base Camp must wait until they are acclimated before making their first foray to Camp I, which is at approximately twenty-one thousand feet. But whereas the hike to Advanced Base Camp was only moderately challenging, the route to Camp I requires skilled mountaineering. This is because mountaineers must cross a vast sheet of ice and climb an ice wall in order to reach their destination.

As mountaineers walk across the ice sheet, their footsteps echo in the distance. Small rocks clatter down on them from above. Ahead they can see the massive ice wall, which must be scaled using fixed ropes. By the time they reach this challenge they are often so tired that they wonder whether they are up to the task. They are also intimidated. As Dickinson explains,

From a distance the ice wall is impressive; seen from its base it is little short of terrifying. The wall stretches up to the sky in a series of gravity-defying seracs . . . and hanging glacial ice. . . . Half of the ice wall is smooth and rounded off like whipped cream, shaped by the Tibetan wind and the eroding effects of sunlight and frost. The remainder consists of shattered pinnacles and gaping scars where avalanches have ripped uneven portions of the face away and dumped the remains on the valley floor.[46]

Avalanches and Falls

As mountaineers traverse the ice wall, they are mindful of the disasters that could confront them and that have come before. For example, during an avalanche (a constant threat on the ice wall), a mass of snow breaks loose from the mountainside and thunders down its slope. Its force alone can kill climbers, but it can also bury them alive. In 1922 seven Sherpas died in an avalanche at the ice wall, and ever since then mountaineers have feared this part of the climb.

Deforestation

Everest's landscape is constantly changing, not only because of fluctuations in weather and temperature but also because of the interference of human beings. Mountaineering efforts have had an enormous impact on Everest's terrain. For instance, in 1999 Sir Edmund Hillary, in his book *View from the Summit*, reported that forests on the mountain have been devastated because of Everest expeditions.

"When I first visited [the south side of Everest] in 1951 the forests were superb—big trees up to an altitude of 13,000 feet and extensive areas of azaleas and juniper shrubs covering the rocky valleys up to 16,000 feet. In 1952 the Swiss Everest expedition cut vast quantities of juniper to burn at their Base Camp and there was still much of this left in 1953. We in our turn burnt the remainder of the Swiss firewood and cut extra ourselves. So the higher valleys after a succession of expeditions quickly became devoid of virtually all shrubs and it is only in more recent years, when the use of firewood in the high valleys has been prohibited, that there has been a modest resurgence of the high-altitude flora."

In order to reach Mt. Everest's summit, mountaineers must climb the ice wall.

However, not everyone struck by an avalanche dies. George Mallory, for example, who was part of the 1922 disaster, lived to tell about it. He later wrote about his experience:

We were startled by an ominous sound, sharp, arresting, violent, and yet somehow soft like an explosion of untamped gunpowder. . . . And then I began to move slowly downwards, inevitably carried on the whole moving surface by a force I was utterly powerless to resist. . . . A wave of snow came over me and I was buried. . . . I thrust out my arms above my head and actually went through some sort of motions of swimming on my back. . . . I struggled in the tumbling snow, unconscious of everything else—until, perhaps, only a few seconds later, I knew the pace was easing up. I felt an increasing pressure about my body. I wondered how tightly I should be squeezed, and then the avalanche came to rest. . . . After a brief struggle, I was standing again, surprised and breathless, in the motionless snow.[47]

Once mountaineers have ascended the ice wall, they generally feel great relief and euphoria. But more dangers await ahead. Above the

A climber ascends the ice. Expedition members must move carefully to avoid avalanches and falls.

wall are mounds of snow so unstable that they could give way at any time, plunging the mountaineer into one of many icy crevasses that lie hidden below. This happened to Reinhold Messner, who describes his experience by saying,

> The snow suddenly gives way under me. . . . I am falling into the depths and experience this fall in slow-motion, strike the walls of the widening crevasse . . . . Suddenly I have support under my feet again. At the same time I know that I am caught, perhaps trapped forever in this crevasse. Cold sweat beads my forehead. Now I am frightened. . . . Also, the snow surface on which I am standing is not firm. . . . Then I discover . . . a ledge the width of two feet in the ice which leads obliquely upwards and is full of snow. That is the way out! . . . I am saved![48]

Climbing in Snow

Because of the constant threat of a dangerous fall, climbers must choose their steps carefully.

This makes climbing in snow a slow process. In many places, mountaineers can progress only two hundred feet in three to four hours. Their feet must be carefully placed, with the crampons jammed into the snow for support. Moving is difficult given the mountaineers' thick clothing and the fact that their goggles can fog or ice up. In addition, mountaineers must think quickly to determine what type of snow they are on because this affects their climbing techniques. As mountaineering experts Don Graydon and Kurt Hanson explain,

> Snow travel is trickier than trail hiking or rock climbing. A rock face stays basically the same, whereas the snowpack undergoes many changes. . . . Snow presents a widely variable surface: seemingly insubstantial . . . powder, consistently firm surface, or the rock hardness of alpine ice. The snowpack can appear to be firm, yet under certain conditions it will suddenly flow in an avalanche and then quickly set to icy hardness.[49]

In some places on Everest, particularly near the summit, mountaineers find deep, powdery snow so fine that it fills in around their feet as they walk, much like sand on a beach. A climber can sink to the waist in this kind of snow. Other places have patches of crumbly limestone rock peeking up from the snow. The mountaineers' crampons can cause this rock to break away, placing them in danger of losing their footing.

The Icefall

There are two particularly unusual regions of terrain on the mountain, the Khumbu Icefall and the Western Cwm. Both are on Everest's south side, one between Base Camp and Camp I and the other between Camp I and Camp II. The Khumbu Icefall begins about a quarter

mile from Base Camp and stretches two miles up the mountain, making it the first mountaineering challenge that expedition members on that side encounter.

The icefall is a region of ice blocks, ice walls, and very tall seracs. It is formed by the Khumbu Glacier, a river of ice that flows at a rate of four feet per day. As the leading edge of this river drops over a cliff, it creates a frozen waterfall, or icefall. But because ice is solid rather than liquid, instead of pouring over the cliff it breaks off in blocks and chunks, which over time form towers and walls. People at the south Base Camp often hear the icefall cracking and roaring, and the

A climber ascends the Khumbu Icefall, a series of ice walls, ice blocks, and seracs formed by the Khumbu Glacier.

ground shakes when large blocks fall. Some mountaineers find this frightening.

Since the icefall never stops moving, its terrain is always changing, forcing climbers to find a new way to cross it. As James Ramsey Ullman explains, "There is no such thing as a 'set' route through the Icefall; for under the gigantic pressures there is constant change in its structure, and each succeeding party of climbers has had to find a path of its own."[50]

Mountaineers must also watch out for chunks of ice falling off the seracs and for new cracks and crevasses that open up suddenly. Sherpas go to the icefall prior to the climbing season to hack pieces off of seracs that look likely to fall on someone. They also knock away snowpacks that might eventually cause an avalanche. But despite their efforts, the region remains perilous.

More than sixty people have died in the Khumbu Icefall since the first mountaineers traveled through the area. Most have been killed by a fall while attempting to get across a crevasse. Mountaineers typically jump over small ones; for medium ones they use ropes and rope ladders to climb down one side and up the other. But many of the icefall's crevasses are more than eight feet wide and seventy feet deep, and these require a more complicated mountaineering technique: walking across aluminum ladders that function as bridges.

Crossing Ladders

A few days before the start of each climbing season, Sherpas determine the best way for mountaineers to cross the icefall and place ladders across any crevasses on the chosen route. Some of these ladders lie horizontally, making a fairly flat bridge, while others are angled with one end higher than the other. For many crevasses, one ladder will span the entire di-

vide. For others, though, two to four ladders must be tied together to make a long enough bridge. Anywhere from seventy to one hundred ladders are required during a season, and a mountaineer typically crosses each of them at least five times while moving up and down Everest as part of the acclimation process.

Mindful of the fact that the icefall is continually moving, the Sherpas anchor the ladders to the ice. In places where a ladder is exceptionally long and/or wobbly, the Sherpas string a guide rope at waist level above the ladder. As with guide ropes elsewhere on the mountain, climbers can clip their harness ropes onto the guide rope so that if they fall off the ladder, the rope will usually stop them—although on a few occasions the rope has not held and the mountaineer has plunged down into the crevasse. Over some of the less daunting crevasses a mountaineer might prefer not to take the time to clip onto the guide rope and instead might merely wrap a hand around the rope for support.

Mountaineers usually walk across the ladders upright, planting each foot on each rung as they slowly progress across the divide. Some climbers, however, find it easier to scoot along horizontal ladders on their bottoms because they have trouble placing their feet so that their boot crampons do not catch on the ladder rungs. A few people are too scared to stand on or scoot across the ladders and prefer to crawl —without looking down, if possible. They are particularly disconcerted by the fact that the ladders are bouncy and often creak and moan during a crossing.

Going through the Khumbu Icefall can be exhausting work. Lene Gammelgaard describes her first time through the region:

> Going up and around ice formations, crossing crevasses, scaling ladders, carefully placing my crampons, balancing, clipping my carabiner [metal ring] to the fixed

A guide rope and ladder help this climber cross a wide crevasse.

ropes. Should I take a fall, there's a fair chance the ropes will break the descent, but I have no desire to test whether these life insurance lines will work, so I gather my concentration instead. . . . This is harsh work! Panting and puffing, . . . hour after hour our team slogs its way upwards. . . . Are we never stopping for a break? Though in the Icefall, there is no decidedly safe spot to rest. But I'm not going to be the wimp, so I drag myself up.[51]

Dangerous Seracs

Mountaineers crossing the icefall also have to deal with dozens of seracs, any of which could possibly tumble as the icefall moves. As mountaineer Eric Shipton once wrote, "One may pass beneath a tottering serac nine times, to be buried by it on the tenth."[52] Many of these towers are more than a hundred feet tall. Gammelgaard describes her experience with one such tower, which her expedition named the Mousetrap:

The Trip Is Dead

Many people have died in the Khumbu Icefall, and when a death occurs some of the people nearby at Base Camp decide to abandon their quest for the summit. This was how 1982 Canadian expedition member Don Serl reacted when three Sherpas died during an avalanche on the icefall. In a diary entry, excerpted in Clint Willis' book *High*, Serl wrote,

"The trip is dead for me and there seems no real reason or cause to revive it. I think we [messed] up badly, and that three lives have been spent teaching us a lesson I doubt we can or will learn. We were far too casual about . . . [the dangers]. . . . I climb for joy, and challenge and danger too, sure, but there's no way I'll be able to enjoy any more of this trip, and there's too little to life to pass it doing things one doesn't enjoy, at least when one has a choice. So it's away for me. I'm going back to climbing between me and the mountain, where I bear the costs, such as they may be, of my errors. Honesty. Directness. Not some horrible situation where three men die and the process can carry on. That's a perversion of any value I care to hold."

A massive leaning tower of ice, which looms above us at a frightening angle. Unfortunately the only way past the Mousetrap is to climb up and over it. I look at the serac apprehensively. It will fall—the only question is when? Only one option: *Go!*—with ice in my stomach—and no stopping. Almost through this overhanging nightmare, one crampon comes loose as I hammer the front points into the ice to climb the remaining vertical feet . . . [but I make it anyway].[53]

Sections of the icefall with many such obstacles were named during Sir Edmund Hillary's 1953 expedition. They include Hellfire Alley, the Atom-Bomb Area, and Hillary's Horror. Mountaineers have typically heard of these icefall areas prior to reaching Everest, fear their danger and difficulty, and feel exhilarated upon making it through each of the famous landmarks. This exhilaration is typically accompanied by an increase in self-confidence, making the icefall an important milestone for first-time Everest climbers. Anatoli Boukreev explains:

> The Icefall . . . is always an important step in the psychological adjustment to the task of climbing Everest. It is jumping off into the unknown. The Icefall is predictably unstable. Each crossing is . . . [a step] in mastering your fear. Your attention is riveted to detail. For several hours you climb, continually crossing gaping crevasses on roped-together bridge ladders, winding ever up through the cascade of shifting blocks of ice the size of houses.[54]

Mountaineers who have not crossed the icefall before typically take more than nine hours to do so. This means that they have to stay overnight at Camp I, just on the other side of the icefall, before heading back to Base Camp. Subsequent icefall crossings, however, usually take less and less time. A person is generally considered physically ready for the final summit assault if he or she can get through the icefall in four to five hours.

The Western Cwm

Another challenging area is the Western Cwm. The word *cwm* (pronounced *koom*) means "valley" in Welsh. It is not actually a valley but an upwardly sloping field of glacial ice and snow, rising two thousand feet from the lower end to the upper. This field is riddled with crevasses that lead down into snow caves. As in the icefield, mountaineers can easily fall into the Cwm's crevasses, so Sherpas mark many of them with bamboo sticks and place ladders over others on a route they have selected prior to the mountaineers' arrival. Some small crevasses, however, are hidden by mounds of snow that could give way at any time. As a result, although the Western Cwm is not as physically demanding as the Khumbu Icefall, traveling through it can be just as dangerous. About her own experience there, Gammelgaard says,

I have to be constantly alert—not being able to see a crevasse doesn't mean it's not there. The altitude, length, and—when the sun pounds down—the heat and the bright light radiating off the snow, ice and valley walls can make passage through the Cwm torture. Add to that the risk of snow and ice avalanches thundering down from the surrounding mountains.[55]

Three mountains surround the Western Cwm: Everest on the left, Lhotse (27,890 feet) in the middle, and Nuptse (25,790 feet) on the right. At the upper edge of the Cwm, at an altitude of 21,300 feet, is a basin where Camp II is located. Camp III is on an area beyond the Cwm known as the Lhotse Face, a 4,000-foot angled wall of ice that requires mountaineers to ascend using ropes anchored to the wall. These first three camps are commonly referred to as

Mountaineers cross the Western Cwm, a sloping field of glacial ice.

the lower camps, with Camps IV through VI referred to as the upper camps. The reason for this difference in designation has to do with the physical demands of high altitudes. The human body can adjust to the altitude levels of the lower camps. The high camps, though, are above such an altitude.

The Lower Camps

Upon reaching any of the lower camps, north or south, mountaineers find nothing but tents with little activity outside of them. The number of tents depends on the amount of terrain flat enough to pitch a tent. At the south Camp II, for example, there is enough room for two hundred people, sleeping three to a tent. Higher up on the mountain, there is room for fewer than a dozen people and only a couple of tents, so mountaineers share sleeping space and stagger their climbs to limit the number of people who will be in any particular camp at one time.

In some camps, Sherpas or mountaineers have to chip the icy ground to make platforms,

or additional flat places, for tents, and even then the tents often stick out slightly over the side of the slope. Mountaineers staying in such places must walk carefully, even with crampons on their boots, and be sure to follow all safety precautions. Even forgetting to put on crampons can be deadly. In 1996 a Taiwanese climber in Camp III slid to his death when he forgot to put on his crampons before going outside in the morning and fell seventy feet into a crevasse.

One particularly difficult place to camp is the North Col, which is the north "shoulder" of Everest. (The word *col* comes from the Latin word *collum*, which means "neck.") As one mountaineer on the 1924 expedition, which helped establish the first camps on the North Col, said, "I can safely say that in two excursions up and down the whole length of the north ridge of Mount Everest I have never seen a single spot affording the 6-foot square level area on which a tent could be pitched without having to build a platform."[56]

There is a corresponding shoulder on the south side of Everest called the South Col, but the terrain there is very different. Whereas on

Background Music

According to Sherry B. Ortner in her book *Life and Death on Mount Everest: Sherpas and Himalayan Mountaineering*, throughout their time on the mountain the Sherpas continually pay their respects to the gods. She describes the way this respect is displayed.

"[The Sherpas] chant mantras [singsong prayers] at almost any time—in the camp, on the climb, in situations of both great danger and routine activity. The sound of Sherpas humming their mantras has been remarked upon by numerous [Western climbers]; it is

virtually the background music of Himalayan expeditions. Similarly, virtually all climbing Sherpas carry with them rice blessed by lamas [holy men] (or, in a pinch, rice over which they themselves recite a blessing) to sprinkle to the gods in times of serious danger. . . . [For example] a climber was knocked down and partly pinned down by a falling block of ice, and was dug out. As he left he passed one of the Sherpas, a young kid who looked under twenty, standing over the hole created by the shifting block, chanting a mantra and tossing sacred rice blessed by a lama."

Camp III (pictured after a snow storm) is located on Lhotse Face, on Everest's south side.

the North Col there is only a narrow strip of land along a mountain ridge, close to a deep crevasse, where a few tents can be crowded together, on the South Col the camp is on a large, flat area with room for several tents spaced comfortably apart.

The two sides are not completely different, however. For example, in either place the terrain does not allow mountaineers to walk far from their tents in order to urinate, a situation that causes sanitation problems because the ice and snow around the tents is the primary source of drinking water. This is a problem elsewhere on the mountain as well. Mountaineer Matt Dickinson reports that he had trouble getting enough water to drink while on Everest "because much of the easiest ice to cut was soiled with urine or other waste."[57]

Inside Lower-Camp Tents

When mountaineers first arrive at any of the camps, they are usually so tired that they can barely wait to collapse into their sleeping bags. Jan Morris offers a typical description of what happens when climbers finally reach their tents:

Wearily they plunge their ice-axes into the snow, unfasten the rope with their stiff cold

Getting Up in the Morning

In their memoirs, Everest mountaineers often complain about how difficult it is to get up and get going on the morning before a climb. In his book *Americans on Everest,* James Ramsey Ullman, a member of the 1963 American expedition, gives an insight into why this is so.

"There was the struggle of simply getting up, of unzipping the sleeping bags, of piling more clothes on over the already large amount worn while sleeping. Half-numb hands fumbled with the opening of cans, the lighting of pressure stoves, the heating of food and liquids. The water, to begin with, was not water but either ice or granulated snow and even when after an endless wait it came to a boil, it was, at these altitudes, not hot but merely tepid. Breakfast over, there was the lacing of boots, the pulling on of still more clothing, the readying of oxygen apparatus, the laborious tying of crampon bindings—the last, despite cold and wind, always an outdoor procedure, lest the sharp crampon spikes rip the floor of the tent. Finally came roping up [attaching ropes to harnesses and packs], the slinging on of packs and oxygen bottles, the adjustment of [oxygen] masks and regulators, the hefting of axes, by which time an average of two hours had passed and breath was coming as hard as after two hours of climbing."

A climber has a meal one morning before an Everest climb.

fingers, and untie . . . the frozen straps of their crampons. . . . Then what a heaving, heavy blowing, bulging, rolling, and twisting ensues! Each tent is no more than three feet high, and it has a narrow sleeve entrance near the ground; into this small hole the tired climber must struggle, wearing awkward windproofs or thick down clothing. There is a maddening struggle with the flapping sleeve of the tent (the snow dripping, all the while, or blowing past in chilling gusts); boots get caught up with nylon tentage; rucksacks [backpacks] have to be dragged in behind.[58]

Quarters inside these tents are extremely tight, yet all cooking, eating, and other activities take place inside to protect mountaineers from the intense cold, wind, and sun. The tents are shared by each mountaineer passing through the camp; the resulting clutter from one mountaineer remains in the tent for another to find. Morris offers a common description of what someone might find upon arrival:

> Inside the tent is probably a little clammy, for it has been empty since the last party went this way. Litter lies about its floor—a bar of chocolate, a packet of breakfast food, a scrap of old newspaper. There is a smell of lemonade powder, wet leather, and chocolate. In one corner is a walkie-talkie set, a tangle of wires and batteries. Once inside this uninviting place, the climber twists himself about laboriously and slowly removes his boots, banging them together to clear them of clinging snow. . . . A few more contortions inside the tent . . . and into his [sleeping] bag, socks, down clothing, gloves and all, the climber gratefully if ungracefully crawls.[59]

From some of the lower camps, mountaineers can see the peak of Everest, and it is an awesome sight. Because of winds that run from west to east across Tibet, the peak has a nearly permanent thirty-mile plume of clouds that streams horizontally from its northeast ridge, also running west to east. These winds are so forceful—some people have estimated that they move at one hundred miles an hour, others at two hundred—that they rip ice crystals off the mountain, then blast and swirl them a great distance from Everest. According to Dickinson,

> The plume has a compelling, hypnotic quality, like the northern lights, or ocean waves breaking on a shore. Once you start watching it, it becomes hard to tear the eyes away, so seductively does it shift and reshape with the passing of time. . . . [Seen from below] the plume is silent, but, like watching someone scream behind soundproof glass, the mind has no trouble imagining the sound that must be accompanying it.[60]

As mountaineers continue on, their fear level mounts. The hardships of life at the lower camps no longer seem as daunting compared to what awaits higher up the mountain.

6 In the Death Zone

The high camps on Everest are in a region known as the Death Zone, which is any part of Everest above 24,606 feet. The term was first used by Swiss physician Edouard Wyss-Durant, who, in his 1952 book *The Mountain World*, first identified the symptoms of altitude sickness. After careful study he determined that no one could survive for very long once he or she passed the 24,606-foot mark.

Living in the Death Zone can be extremely dangerous and exhausting. Campsites are bleak, and the altitude makes many people feel sick and depressed. Consequently, after spending time in this region, many mountaineers find themselves wondering why they ever decided to come to Everest at all. Matt Dickinson reflects the common sentiment when he describes the north Camp V, at 25,196 feet:

> The platform [where I pitched my tent] was littered with the shredded remains of abandoned tents, with strips of fabric blowing in the wind. Pieces of rope, half-buried foil packets of food, and remnants of clothing were embedded in almost every inch of ice. Sharp metal snow stakes were sticking out at crazy angles, attached to lines that went nowhere. Large areas of ice were stained yellow from urine, and frozen feces were abundantly scattered around. This mess had obviously been accumulating year after year, as expeditions abandoned their gear, or had it destroyed in storms. It was a depressing location, soiled and spiritless; I was already looking forward to getting out of Camp V and we had only just arrived.[61]

Besides the dreary accommodations, the Death Zone's high altitudes create numerous problems. Some climbers barely manage to feed themselves upon arriving in camp. One mountaineer tells how much effort it takes for someone to prepare food in the Death Zone:

> On arrival one crawls into the tent, so completely exhausted that for perhaps three-quarters of an hour one just lies in a sleeping-bag and rests. Then . . . one member of the party with groans and pantings and frequent rests crawls out of his bag, out of the tent and a few yards to a neighbouring patch of snow, where he fills two big aluminium pots with snow; his companion with more panting and groans sits up in bed, lights the . . . cooker and opens some tea, sugar and condensed milk, a tin of sardines or beef and a box of biscuits. Presently both are again ensconced in their sleeping-bags side by side, with the cooker doing its indifferent best to produce half a pot of warm water from each piled pot of powdery snow.[62]

Second Thoughts

At this point some climbers reconsider their intent to summit and experience a strong urge to leave camp and go back down the mountain. This is the mind's response to the dangerous altitude. The mountaineer's survival is at risk, and the instinctive response is to flee to a safer altitude. For example, when American mountaineer Ed Webster reached the Death Zone, he found himself thinking,

> What I would [give] to be transported virtually anywhere else from the hell of this frozen world! I imagined warm, white sandy beaches, sunny Colorado; the normal everyday things in life: going for a walk, eating dinner with friends. Things I'd too often taken for granted. As soon as I escaped from this mountain, I would revel in the mundane.[63]

Such thoughts can grow worse as mountaineers go higher because the stresses of the altitude increase in intensity. It is more difficult for mountaineers to move, breathe, and think; thirst and fatigue are extreme. Climbers cannot get their water hot, no matter how long they boil it. In the early years of Everest expeditions, cookstoves would not even work at this altitude because of pressure changes in the air.

Although the mountaineers anticipate these types of problems before leaving for Everest, many find them difficult to bear once they are on the mountain. For example, while in the north Camp VI at 27,230 feet, Reinhold Messner thought to himself,

> How does one live at this height? I am no longer living, I am only vegetating. . . . I can make clear decisions only very slowly. They are influenced by my tiredness and breathing difficulties. . . . Although I have not been able to prepare any really hot drinks, because water boils at a lower temperature on account of the height, I still keep on melting snow. Pot after pot. I drink soup and salt tea. It is still too little. I am not very hungry. I must force myself to eat. Also I don't know what to eat without making myself sick. Should I open this tin of sardines now or something else? The slightest effort requires time, energy and attention. . . . I decide on cheese and bread, chicken in curry sauce, a freeze-dried ready to serve meal which I mix with lukewarm water. I stick the empty packet under the top of my sleeping bag. I shall need it during the

A Wretched Existence

Frank S. Smythe had a particularly hard time spending the night at the highest camp during his 1933 expedition. Breathing only the air on the mountain, his throat grew dry and sore, and his lungs had difficulty functioning. Every task was exhausting. Smythe's description is quoted in James Ramsey Ullman's book *Kingdom of Adventure.*

"No words can give any idea of our wretched existence in the little tent at a height of twenty-seven thousand four hundred feet. The cooking arrangements were inadequate, the solid methylated fuel took an hour or longer to melt a saucepan of snow and then failed completely to raise it to the boil. . . . It was only with difficulty that we could force food down our sore throats, and so lethargic were we that every movement, even the simplest action, cost us an enormous effort. It was all we could do, for instance, to pull off our wind jackets, and once in our sleeping-bags it was next to impossible to extricate ourselves, as every movement, however small, made us gasp and gasp for breath. It was a horrible night."

night to pee in. It takes me more than half an hour to choke down the [meal].[64]

A Sleepless Night

Mountaineers try not to stay more than one night in any of the upper camps, although they may have to if the weather turns so bad that they cannot leave. Moreover, as with the lower camps, they move back down the mountain after climbing up to an upper camp in order to acclimate themselves. When the mountaineers are fully acclimated and therefore feel relatively fit at the high camps, they usually—under advice from their expedition guides—decide they are ready for their assault on the peak. When this happens they work their way up to the highest camp on either side of the mountain and sleep there for one night before beginning their assault.

Being in the highest camp intensifies the mountaineers' physical and mental discomfort, making it difficult for them to get any rest. Mountaineer Ray Lambert, who spent the night at 27,500 feet before his assault, describes his 1952 expedition's difficulties sleeping:

> It was a glacial night. . . . Our muscles stiffened and those of the face became fixed as if from an injection of anaesthetic. Slowly the cold penetrated the bones themselves. There was no question of sleep: the wind and the growling avalanches kept us awake. . . . We were overtaken by a consuming thirst, which we could not appease. . . . The gusts of wind made our heads whirl; it seemed to us that we took off with them into space.[65]

Many people, even those who have not used it earlier, find that they can not sleep in

---

Tent Fires

Because it is necessary to cook meals in a tent, fire is always a danger on an Everest expedition. In his book *Americans on Everest*, James Ramsey Ullman describes a tent fire caused by the carelessness of two climbers suffering from altitude sickness.

"As Lute [one of the climbers] was attaching a fresh butane cylinder to one of the two stoves he was using, there was a sudden great whoosh and a burst of flame filled the tent. Both men's beards and eyebrows were singed. Barry's plastic oxygen mask was consumed in one blinding second. And in the next, with the fire still burning, the little tent was filled with acrid white smoke. Said Barry: 'Panic gripped us. Lute struggled toward the zippered entrance, and I tried to smother the flames with

my sleeping bag; but my legs were still inside it and I could get no leverage. Meanwhile the fire was feeding on the air in the tent, soon exhausting it, and our lungs were aching. I was groping desperately for a knife to cut through the tent wall, when Lute managed to tear open the zipper and literally dived outside. His momentum was so great that he almost pitched down the steep slope. . . . I was on his heels. We snatched the flaming stove from the tent, doused it in the snow, and soon the fire had died in the thin air.' The tent and most of its contents were all right; they did not go up in flames. But the spasm of violent action was almost more than the two men could take, and for several minutes they sagged, gasping and choking, on their hands and knees in the snow."

Climbers make their final assault on the peak.

the Death Zone without supplemental oxygen. But even though the oxygen helps them fall asleep, they are jolted awake when the bottle needs to be replaced or when a malfunction in the oxygen delivery system occurs because of the extreme cold.

Turning Back

Regardless of how tired they are, however, on summit day the mountaineers must muster enough strength to make it the rest of the way to the top of Everest—or back down to a lower camp. Upon waking in the morning, a few of them find that they simply do not have the physical strength or the mental will to continue.

It is never easy to make the decision to turn around, but mountaineers are taught to do so if their fatigue is so great that it would jeopardize their ability to go back down the mountain after reaching the summit. According to Beck Weathers, "One of the things you must honestly ask yourself on a mountain—it is a moral obligation to your fellow climbers—is, with this step, how much do I have left? Can I still turn around and get back down to safety?"[66]

Mountaineers are supposed to make this decision themselves, but it is often difficult for them to do so because of the confusion and poor judgement that can occur at high altitude. As Sir Edmund Hillary says, "At 29,000 feet no one, not even the best of them, is fully mentally balanced and can be relied on to make correct decisions all

Frozen Boots

One of the greatest difficulties faced by climbers while ascending the mountain is frozen boots. Above Base Camp, climbers often sleep with their boots on to keep them warmed up and ready for the next morning. When they do not, they typically have to heat up their boots before they can put them on. This was the case for Geoffrey Bruce and George Finch during their 1922 attempt to reach the summit; they had to hold their boots over lit candles to soften them up enough to put them on. Another climber who suffered the same fate was Eric Shipton, whose boots froze during a 1933 expedition while he was camping just fourteen hundred feet below Everest's summit. At this altitude the thawing process was long, as was the time it took for him to put on all of the clothes necessary for his climb to the summit. In his book *Climbing Everest: An Anthology*, editor Geoffrey Broughton quotes Shipton's description of the thawing and dressing process.

"Thawing our boots was the longest job; they were like lumps of rock. We had intended taking them to bed with us to keep them soft, but, like so many good resolutions made below, this had not been done. But by holding them over candle-flames we managed to make the uppers sufficiently pliable, and, with a tremendous effort, to force our feet, already encased in four or five pairs of socks, into them. For the rest we each wore two pairs of long woollen pants, seven sweaters and a loosely-fitting windproof with a hood that went over a . . . [soft] helmet. Our hands were protected by one pair of thick woollen mitts covered with a pair of sheepskin gauntlets [a long glove with a wide cuff]. I felt about as suitably equipped for delicate rock-climbing as a fully rigged deep-sea diver for dancing a tango."

of the time."[67] Therefore, in the Death Zone mountaineers almost always climb in pairs or groups, so they can monitor one another to make sure everyone is in good shape.

Interestingly, although a few mountaineers feel a sense of disappointment when they turn back, many feel relief. Again, this is the mind's attempt at self-preservation; the relief exists to encourage the mountaineer to continue his flight to safety. It is only afterward, back in Base Camp, that some of the mountaineers begin to experience disappointment. Others, though, never regret their decision, knowing that even if they had reached the summit they never would have returned alive. Edward Norton was one such person. He turned back at 28,126 feet—with no more than 900 feet to go—during his 1924 summit assault on the north side, but he later wrote,

I feel that I ought to record the bitter feeling of disappointment which I should have experienced on having to acknowledge defeat with the summit so close; yet I cannot conscientiously say that I felt it much at the time. Twice now I have had thus to turn back on a favourable day when success had appeared possible, yet on neither occasion did I feel the sensations appropriate to the moment. This I think is a psychological effect of great altitudes; the better qualities of ambition and will to conquer seem dulled to nothing and one turns downhill with little feeling other than the relief that the strain and efforts of climbing are finished.[68]

Norton's turning back while struggling to climb to the summit was not unusual. With every step the goal becomes more daunting—which means, ironically, that the closer the mountaineers come to the peak, the more likely it is that they will turn back.

Assaulting the Summit

Reaching the summit from the highest camp on either side of the mountain usually takes a climber twelve to fourteen hours. Mountaineers typically embark for the summit before midnight, reach it around noon, and are back down in camp before midnight to avoid spending a night unsheltered and alone. As long as they are moving they can stay warm and alert. If they stop they could freeze and die.

Before leaving, mountaineers grab fresh oxygen tanks and strap on their oxygen masks. Some have been using supplemental oxygen for days prior to this moment, but others have reserved it only for the final assault. A few climb to the peak without any supplemental oxygen at all.

Those who do use oxygen find that it isolates them from their fellow expedition members because it is impossible to talk while wearing an oxygen mask. Nonetheless, most do not find this upsetting; in fact, some find it pleasant. For instance, Dougal Haston says, "There's something surrealistic about being alone high on Everest at . . . [3 A.M.]. No end to the strange beauty of the experience. Alone, enclosed in a mask with the hard rattle of your breathing echoing in your ears."[69]

Alone or with a group, being on Everest in the early hours of the morning is an amazing experience. Perhaps the best description of what it is like to leave for the peak in the dark is that of Beck Weathers, whose assault began on a night when it was ten degrees below zero:

Besides our headlamps, there was no artificial light anywhere, which allowed the stars

above us to shine with incredible brilliance. You even could see them reflected in that cold blue ice beneath your feet. They seemed so close, as if you could just reach up and pluck them from the heavens. . . . Our pace was that slow, rhythmic, metronome-like gait ingrained in the frame of my being through years of prior climbing. With each step those knives [on the bottom of my boots] bite into the ice with a distinctive *creech-ch-ch*. As you move and shift your weight in the cold, the metal in your boots and the bindings on your pack squeak in response. . . . You travel in a private bubble of light from your headlamp, the rest of the world is as lost to you as if you were alone on the face of the moon. All you have to do is step and rest, step and rest —hour after hour after endless hour.[70]

Weathers, Haston, and many other mountaineers have described feeling a sense of peace while assaulting the peak. Some people believe that this feeling comes from the use of supplemental oxygen, perhaps because it relieves the suffering that the brain has been experiencing throughout the lower part of the climb. Jon Krakauer is one person who believes his sense of peace on the mountain came from a bottle. He says,

Bottled oxygen does not make the top of Everest feel like sea level. . . . I had to stop and draw three or four lungfuls of air before each ponderous step. . . . But the bottled oxygen conferred other benefits. . . . I enjoyed a strange, unwarranted sense of calm. The world beyond the rubber [oxygen] mask was stupendously vivid but seemed not quite real, as if a movie were being projected in slow motion across the front of my goggles. I felt drugged, disengaged, thoroughly insulated from external stimuli. I had to remind myself over and over that there was 7,000 feet of sky on either side, that everything was at stake here, that I would pay for a single bungled step with my life.[71]

Climbers who do not use oxygen tanks report no such sense of peace. Their minds are too busy struggling to focus, their bodies too busy struggling to take each breath, for them to feel relaxed. Reinhold Messner describes his own difficulties while foregoing supplemental oxygen during his assault:

While climbing I watch only the foot making the step. Otherwise there is nothing. The air tastes empty, not stale, just empty and rough. My throat hurts. While resting I let myself droop, ski sticks and legs take the weight of my upper body. Lungs heave.

On their way to the peak, climbers may encounter frozen corpses like this one. More than 140 mountaineers have died climbing Mt. Everest.

Devoid of Life

No plants or animals live in Everest's Death Zone because, like humans, they cannot exist for long in the region's thin air and cold temperatures. One small creature, however, is able to live just two thousand feet below the Death Zone: the Attid spider, which makes its home in the cracks between mountain rocks. In addition, birds called chough have been spotted at twenty-seven thousand feet, vultures at twenty-five thousand feet, and crows at twenty-one thousand feet. All of these birds are scavengers and often feed on dead bodies. Scientists believe that they fly up to the Death Zone to feed and then immediately fly back down to a lower altitude, just as climbers move up and down Everest during an expedition.

For a time I forget everything. Breathing is so strenuous that no power to think remains. Noises from within me drown out all external sounds.[72]

Facing Death

Sometimes, however, the assault experience is shattered by the sight of a corpse. As the ice melts and the snow tumbles debris down the mountain, the bodies of people who have lost their lives on Everest can be revealed. More than 140 Western climbers and Sherpas have died on the mountain at various points along various routes to the summit. In many cases their bodies are not found at the time but emerge a season or two later. Although corpses do not decay at the highest altitudes, wind can wear away skin and tissue. This means that bodies only recently uncovered by shifting snow or resting in a place sheltered from the winds look intact while those exposed to the elements for long periods are little more than skeletons.

One of the most talked-about corpses among mountaineers is that of German climber Hannelore Schmatz, who died on Everest in 1979. Although this blonde-haired corpse has now been removed, for many years it sat beside the trail at 27,600 feet, appearing to greet climbers as they passed. Norwegian mountaineer Arne Naess Jr. describes his encounter with it:

I can't escape the sinister guard. . . . She sits leaning against her pack, as if taking a short break. A woman with her eyes wide open and her hair waving in each gust of wind. . . . She summited, but died descending. Yet it feels as if she follows me with her eyes as I pass by. Her presence reminds me that we are here on the conditions of the mountain.[73]

Today it is not uncommon to see a corpse—or a mound of snow that climbers have used to cover a corpse—while on a well-traveled trail. Most bodies are left on the mountain because of the dangers and difficulties of retrieving them. Moreover, Sherpas believe that it is bad luck to remove a body from the mountain.

Difficult Spots

Seeing corpses on the trail reminds mountaineers of the dangers of their ascent, and several points along the assault route are so challenging that they make most mountaineers consider turning back. One such point is an area of rock known as the Yellow Band. Made of crumbly limestone and covered only lightly with patches of snow, it is at a place so steep that mountaineers cannot stop to remove their crampons before reaching it, even though crampons are not meant to be used while traversing terrain that is primarily rock. As Matt Dickinson explains, "[Climbing with crampons on rock] is like trying to climb stairs on stilts. The spiked fangs act like an unwanted platform sole, elevating the foot away from any real contact with the rock. Using crampons on rock greatly increases the risk of a misplaced foothold or a twisted ankle."[74]

Great care must be taken while climbing the Yellow Band to ensure that the mountaineer does not fall, but there are even more troublesome spots awaiting mountaineers who decide to try for the summit via unconventional routes. Occasionally a team of mountaineers will decide that the established north and south assault paths are not challenging enough, so they climb for the peak from a different part of Everest. In nearly every case this has led to disaster. For example, in 1975, British climbers Chris Bonington, Dougal Haston, and Doug Scott became the first people to climb Everest from the southwest, a course that involves extremely heavy snow and difficult terrain. In doing so, they took so long that they were caught outside when night came and almost froze to death while waiting to hike back down the mountain. Haston later described their long ascent:

> Progress? The word seemed almost laughable as I moved more and more slowly. A first step and in [the snow] up to the waist. Attempts to move upward only resulted in a deeper sinking motion. Time for new techniques: step up, sink in, then start clearing away the slope in front . . . and eventually you pack enough [snow] together to be able to move a little further and sink in only to your knees.[75]

Because these unconventional paths are so dangerous, most people stick to the established assault routes on the north and south, where, as at lower altitudes, guide ropes lead the way to the top. However, winds and soil erosion have damaged the oldest of these ropes and their anchors. Sherpas and expedition leaders often attempt to repair or replace the damaged ropes, but because they, like the climbers, are so exhausted by the time they reach this point they often do not do a good job. This means that even when mountaineers are clipped on to guide ropes, they could still fall when an old rope breaks or a section of the guide rope is missing.

Eroding Terrain

Because the mountaineers all climb on the same path, any rocky areas along the route are subject to erosion from boots and ice axes. This means that although the traditional routes to Everest's peak are the same each year, the terrain is not. Consequently, even a mountaineer who has summitted before must be alert to new areas of crumbling or slippery rocks.

One section of the assault route on the south that has changed significantly over the years is also the most strenuous part of the climb: the Hillary Step, named for Sir Edmund Hillary, the first person to climb it. A vertical tower of rock, ice, and snow approximately ten meters high, it was first surmounted by Sir Edmund Hillary and Tenzing Norgay during their successful 1953 assault. Hillary describes his experience climbing his namesake:

> Ahead of me loomed the great rock step which we had observed from far below. . . . I gazed up at the forty feet of rock with some concern. To climb it directly at nearly 29,000 feet would be a considerable chal-

lenge. . . . Clinging to the rock was a great ice cornice. . . . Under the effects of gravity, the ice had broken away from the rock and a narrow crack ran upward. . . . I eased my way into the crack, facing the rock. I jammed my crampons into the ice behind me and then wriggled my way upward using every little handhold I could find. Puffing for breath, I made steady height—the ice was holding—and forty feet up I pulled

The Hillary Step (pictured) is the most challenging climb on the southern assault route.

In the Death Zone 81

myself out of the crack onto the top of the rock face. I had made it![76]

The Hillary Step has always required the best rock-climbing skills at a point when most mountaineers are almost completely exhausted. However, over the years, because the rock has eroded considerably, it has become less and less challenging. James Ramsey Ullman noted the changes as early as 1963:

Apparently the years . . . wrought changes in its structure, for now, mercifully, [the Hillary Step] created no major obstacle. . . . There was still the rock on the left, the snow on the right . . . but there was no steepness now; only humps and hummocks [small rises], each just a little higher than the one before it; and there were ten of them, fifteen, twenty—rising, rising. Some were of rock, some of snow, some a mixture of both.

Mountaineers at the top of the Hillary Step prepare to summit Mt. Everest.

Then there was no more mixture, no more rock, but only snow; only a rounded white dome curved slightly above them.[77]

This snow dome existed in Hillary's time as well, and it continues to exist today, marking the last few feet before the summit itself. When mountaineers reach this point, they know that they are almost at their goal. The excitement that this causes often gives them the burst of energy necessary to go the rest of the way up. Some mountaineers, however, have had to be helped by other expedition members for the last few steps, too physically and mentally tired to make it by themselves. Still others find that they cannot summon the physical and mental energy necessary to go a step farther even when helped. Despite the many challenges, most climbers press on toward the ultimate goal of reaching Everest's peak.

Celebration and Descent

When climbers do reach the summit, their sense of joy can be great. A goal has been reached, a challenge met, and fears conquered. It is a time for congratulations and celebrations. Some mountaineers open their packs and bring out special food to eat or drink or a memorable poem to read to mark the occasion. However, because of the extreme fatigue that mountaineers are feeling by this time, many find their enthusiasm subdued. For example, Doug Scott said of his own moment on the peak,

All the world lay before us. That summit was everything and more that a summit should be. My . . . [climbing] partner became expansive, his face broke out in a broad happy smile and we stood there hugging each other and thumping each other's backs. The implications of reaching the top of the highest mountain in the world surely had some bearings on our feelings, . . . but I can't say it was that strong. I can't say either that I felt any relief that the struggle was over. In fact, in some ways it seemed a shame that it was, for we had been fully programmed [to climb] and now we had to switch off and go back into reverse. But not yet, for the view was so staggering, the disappearing sun so full of colour that the setting held us in awe.[78]

Other mountaineers, like Scott's climbing partner, are overwhelmed by the view from the top of the world. Matt Dickinson says,

My overwhelming impression was of stupendous height. Even though it is surrounded by other gigantic 8,000-meter . . . peaks like Lhotse and Nuptse, Everest does not compete with them once you are on its peak—it dominates them completely. Everest does not jostle for position in the heart of the Himalayas, it presides over its lowlier cousins with effortless majesty.[79]

It is traditional to take photographs on the summit, not only of the view but of the mountaineers there. Expedition members take pictures of one another to prove that they made it to the top. Many also leave mementos on the summit. These two traditions—carrying special items to the peak and photographing each other on the summit—date back to the first two climbers to stand on the peak. When Tenzing Norgay and Sir Edmund Hillary reached the top, Norgay placed flags representing the United Nations, India, Nepal, and Great Britain on the summit. He also left pieces of chocolate and other foods as gifts for the gods. Once he was done, Hillary placed a small crucifix on the summit as a favor for another climber who had turned back before reaching the peak. Then he took photographs to show that he really had reached his goal. Hillary and Norgay found the peak deserted, but today a battered aluminum survey pole marks the highest spot on Earth, placed there by the Chinese government in 1975.

Hurrying Down

After a few moments of celebration, most mountaineers begin to experience dread or even fear. This is because they know they must still get back down the mountain, and they feel so exhausted from their ascent that they cannot even imagine how they will summon the strength for their descent. Jon Krakauer represents many mountaineers when he says,

A mountaineer takes in the view from the peak of Mt. Everest.

Reaching the top of Everest was supposed to trigger a surge of intense elation; against long odds, after all, I had just attained a goal I'd coveted since childhood. But the summit was really only the halfway point. Any impulse I might have felt toward self-congratulations was extinguished by overwhelming apprehension about the long, dangerous descent that lay ahead.[80]

The majority of Everest deaths occur during the descent rather than the ascent because, as Beck Weathers says, "Climbing down a mountain is a lot more dangerous than climbing up. If you're going to get yourself killed, that's generally when it happens."[81] What makes the descent so dangerous is that people who have reached the summit typically do not have enough energy left to descend safely. They are so tired that their tendency is to stumble and fall forward, and while heading downhill such a fall could start a tumble that would be hard to stop. As Dickinson reports,

For me, the descent [of Everest] was the most nerve-jangling part of the nightmare.

. . . Down-climbing is always more dangerous than going up. The body is facing away from the . . . [mountain], so that the chances of an accidental slip become much more likely than they are on the ascent. Shod in the infernal crampons, skittering and clattering across the loose, frozen slabby rock of the North Face, I several times felt myself close to plummetting down the 10,000-foot precipice.[82]

Adding to the danger are the effects of being at high altitude for so long. By the time mountaineers reach the peak, their minds and bodies are urging them to return to a lower altitude as quickly as possible. If they do not get down quickly, they will begin to experience the most severe symptoms of altitude sickness and could collapse and die on the mountain. The risk of developing altitude-related mental confusion while descending from the peak is also high; mountaineers experiencing this condition can easily veer from the correct path or irrationally sit down with no thought of getting back up again. Reinhold Messner speaks of the latter danger:

Trash

Even near the summit of Everest, trash is a particularly difficult problem. Many expeditions have left behind a variety of refuse, including discarded equipment and human waste, because of the effort it would take to haul it back down the mountain. In 1999 Sir Edmund Hillary commented about this problem in his book *View from the Summit*.

"Everest has become an appalling junk heap with masses of empty oxygen bottles, torn tents, tin cans and even a few bodies as well. Regrettably our own expedition [in 1953] was one of the first to set this miserable example and it is not much of an excuse to say we didn't know any better in those days. Fortunately, matters are slowly changing. Quite a few expeditions [now] make considerable efforts to remove their rubbish off the mountain. Some even remove other people's rubbish. So a sense of environmental responsibility is slowly creeping in."

My will-power is dulled. The longer I climb the less important the goal seems to me, the more indifferent I become to myself. My attention has diminished, my memory is weakened. My mental fatigue is now greater than the bodily. It is so pleasant to sit doing nothing—and therefore so dangerous. Death through exhaustion is—like death through freezing—a pleasant one.[83]

During the descent, some people also begin to hallucinate from the effects of being at such a high altitude for so long. For example, as Krakauer struggled to descend from the peak during rising winds, he had a moment in which his mind played tricks on him. As he explains,

I was so far beyond ordinary exhaustion that I experienced a queer detachment from my body, as if I were observing my descent from a few feet overhead. I imagined that I was dressed in a green cardigan and wingtips [shoes]. And although the gale was generating a windchill in excess of seventy [degrees] below zero Fahrenheit, I felt strangely, disturbingly warm.[84]

Even when the mind remains able to cope with the descent, the body can start to give out. Getting to the peak is such an effort that the descent to the nearest campsite seems to take an eternity. Every step is an effort, every breath a struggle. Moreover, if people linger too long on the summit, they run the risk of running out of supplemental oxygen before they make it back to camp.

People who have assaulted the summit while under the influence of supplemental oxygen have become highly dependent on it by this time. This means that when the oxygen runs out, they will experience the effects of the altitude so severely that breathing difficulties and altitude sickness will come on almost immediately. In contrast, climbers who have summitted without oxygen experience the same degree of labored breathing and feelings of sickness going down as they did going up.

Sudden Storms

Another danger of the descent is the risk of getting caught in a storm. Because it takes so long to make it to the summit and back, Everest's notoriously unstable weather has plenty of time to change. The jet stream that brings storms to the mountain's upper altitudes can suddenly shift, and the speed of its winds can sweep clouds onto the peak very quickly. As mountaineer Eric Shipton once said, "I have never known anything like the suddenness of those Everest storms. They arrived out of perfect stillness, without any warning, and at the full height of their power."[85]

Therefore when mountaineers are standing on the summit under a clear sky, they cannot assume that the weather will stay that way. They must remember that a dangerous storm could hit at any moment, either while they are on the peak or during their descent. Expedition leaders warn climbers not to linger too long on the summit, but given their excitement, some mountaineers forget the warnings. This was the case for climbers on a 1996 commercial expedition during which many members perished. They had been told to spend only fifteen minutes on the summit, yet they had been so excited that they spent forty-five minutes instead. During their descent, oxygen supplies ran out and the climbers were caught in a storm. One of the expedition members who had remembered the warning and returned on time, thereby escaping the danger, later said, "People mistakenly think it was the storm that caused

Members of the 1996 expedition just before they were caught in a sudden storm. Such violent storms make the descent from the peak very dangerous.

the problem. It wasn't the storm that caused the problem; it was the time."[86]

Once the storm hit, the mountaineers caught in it could not see anything. Climber Neal Beidleman described their plight, saying, "It was like being inside of a milk bottle. The winds were blowing . . . anywhere from . . . forty miles an hour up to maybe gusts of eighty or more. They were enough to knock us off our feet many times."[87] Stumbling blindly through the snow,

Beidleman had great difficulty descending to the nearest campsite during the storm. It was only luck that brought him to a point where he could make out a few landmarks and find the tents.

Getting Lost

Even in good weather it can be difficult to find the correct path down the unroped parts of the mountain, largely due to the mental confusion that mountaineers are experiencing by this point. Krakauer had such an experience as he rushed down the mountain to avoid the 1996 storm. He later recalled,

> I descended a few hundred feet down a broad, gentle snow gully without incident, but then things began to get sketchy. The route meandered through outcroppings of broken shale [rock] blanketed with six inches of fresh snow. Negotiating the puzzling, infirm terrain demanded unceasing concentration, an all-but-impossible feat in my punch-drunk state. Because the wind had erased the tracks of the climbers who'd gone down before me, I had difficulty determining the correct route.[88]

Losing one's way is such a risk—even in good weather—that many mountaineers become preoccupied with studying the terrain during their ascent so that they will not make a wrong turn during their descent. As Krakauer says,

> In the morning, on the way up, I'd made a point of continually studying the route on this [unmarked] part of the mountain, frequently looking down to pick out landmarks that would be helpful on the descent, compulsively memorizing the terrain: "remember to turn left at the buttress that looks like a ship's prow. Then follow that skinny line of snow until it curves sharply to the right." This was something I . . . forced myself to go through every time I climbed [any mountain], and on Everest it may have saved my life.[89]

Krakauer got to his tent before the full brunt of the storm hit. But another mountaineer caught in the storm, Beck Weathers, did not escape the weather's wrath during his descent. Caught in a blizzard and unable to see, he collapsed facedown in the snow and fell unconscious; several hours later he suddenly revived and started walking without any sense of direction. Fortunately,

Devising Signals

During the deadly 1996 storm, one mountaineer used a radio to say goodbye to his wife in New Zealand as he died near the peak. In earlier times, though, mountaineers near the peak had to rely on visual signals to communicate with people down the mountain. For example, in searching for two lost climbers, the 1924 expedition agreed on a system whereby blankets would be arranged in various patterns to send messages from one location on the mountain to another. Mountaineer John Hazard was four thousand feet above the rest of his expedition when he laid six blankets on the snow in the shape of a cross. To the men waiting below with binoculars, this meant that Hazard had abandoned all hope of finding the missing climbers.

he stumbled into a group of tents, where other climbers eventually helped him down to Camp I. Too weak and frostbitten to continue on to Base Camp, Weathers rode a helicopter off the mountain from Camp I, the highest altitude to which such a craft had ever flown.

Bivouacs

Many people say it is a miracle that Weathers lived to tell about his experience. Climbers caught outside overnight during a storm usually do not survive, and the few people who have

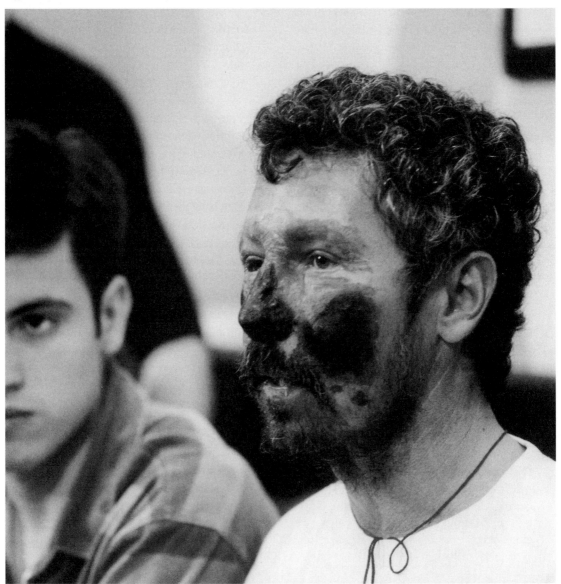

Beck Weathers (right) miraculously survived the 1996 storm, although he still suffered facial wind burns and frostbite.

managed to do so report that their experience was terrifying. As Peter Habeler, who was caught in a storm near the summit of Everest in 1978, explains,

> What it means to survive a stormy night at such an altitude can only be imagined by somebody who has personally experienced it. Even under the most favourable circumstances every step at that altitude demands a colossal effort of will. You must force yourself to make every movement, reach for every handhold. You are perpetually threatened by a leaden, deadly fatigue. If you are exposed in such a situation to a storm, with squalls which reach a maximum speed of 130 kilometers [80 miles] an hour; if a heavy snowdrift sets in, so dense that you can no longer see your hand in front of your face, your position becomes practically hopeless. You must cling on firmly to the ice in order not to be hurled off the mountain. Everybody is left to his own resources. If something happens to you, help is out of the question. Everybody has enough to do in trying to save themselves.[90]

To increase their chances of survival, mountaineers try to cut a hole into a bank of ice or snow using their ice axe and hollow out the hole—also called a bivouac—to protect themselves from the wind. Close to the summit, though, it is unlikely that a climber will find ice or snow soft enough to chisel or the energy required to hack away even the smallest hole. Still, a few men have managed to dig such holes and survive under very difficult conditions at the highest altitudes. Often they worked as a team, rubbing each other for warmth and talking to each other to keep from falling asleep, knowing that if they stopped moving they would freeze to

death. Combined body warmth is an asset inside a bivouac; only a few solo climbers have ever survived overnight in a storm. In fact, the only person to have survived in a bivouac alone above 27,800 feet was British climber Stephen Venables in 1988.

Reaching Safety

When mountaineers do reach their tents after a successful summit assault, their sense of exhilaration can be even greater than when they reached the peak itself. Krakauer expresses the common sentiment when he tells of his own return to the highest south camp:

> Fifteen minutes of dicey, fatiguing crampon work brought me safely to the bottom of the incline . . . and another ten minutes after that I was in camp myself. I lunged into my tent with my crampons still on, zipped the door tight, and sprawled across the frost-covered floor too tired to even sit upright. For the first time I had a sense of how wasted I really was: I was more exhausted than I'd ever been in my life. But I was safe. . . . The others would be coming into camp soon. We'd . . . done it. We'd climbed Everest.[91]

After staying a day or two in the highest camp, mountaineers begin their descent to the lower camps. If the weather is bad they might stay longer in the Death Zone, but this is dangerous because their bodies can handle very little time at such a high altitude. Therefore, even exhausted climbers usually try to get down the mountain as quickly as possible. Along the way to Base Camp they stop at each camp they encounter to rest and rehydrate themselves, but only for as short a time as

Sherpa Tenzing Norgay, who, with Sir Edmund Hillary, became the first mountaineer to reach the summit in 1953, describes his climbing partner in his book *Tiger of the Snows:*

"Hillary was a wonderful climber—especially on snow and ice, with which he had much practice in New Zealand—and had great strength and endurance. Like many men of action, and especially the British, he did not talk much, but he was, nevertheless, a fine-cheerful companion; and he was popular with the Sherpas, because in things like food and equipment he always shared whatever he had. I suppose we made a funny-looking pair, he and I, with Hillary about six feet three inches tall and myself some seven inches shorter. But we were not worrying about that. What was important was that, as we climbed together and became used to each other, we were becoming a strong and confident team."

possible. For some climbers, this is a few hours; for others, a day or two.

A Satisfying End

Mountaineers also spend a limited amount of time in Base Camp once they return from their summit assault. Their expedition is over; it is time to go home. They rest just long enough to gather their personal belongings and gain the strength to make the trek back to Katmandu. Once there, they are usually interviewed by Elizabeth Hawley, who has lived in Katmandu for more than twenty years. Years ago she worked as Sir Edmund Hillary's secretary, but today she is a journalist and historian who maintains a detailed record of events on the Himalayan mountains. She also verifies "firsts" and provides information on them and on mountaineering disasters to reporters throughout the world.

Her interviews reveal that many mountaineers profit emotionally from their experiences on Everest. Regardless of whether they reached the summit, climbers often gain important insights about themselves and about life. For example, Frank S. Smythe, who went on expeditions during the 1930s, once wrote,

In mountaineering, and on Mount Everest in particular, a man sees himself for what he is. He learns the value of comradeship and of service. In the bitter cold and blasting winds he sees life for the grand thing it is. He learns the value of a superlatively fit body, of a mind inspired by no motives of selfish gain but by achievement for the sake of achievement. An Everest expedition brings a man into contact with the simple and happy things in life. The cares of civilization slip away. . . . Life becomes simple, and the simplicity is the soulmate of happiness. Never does a plateful of soup and mutton taste so well as it does after a hard day's work in the open. Nature is honest, there is no meanness in her composition, she has no time for fools, there is no place in her code for weaklings and degenerates. Out of her strength we gather our own strength. And it is good be to strong, to be able to endure, not as a brute beast, but as a thinking man imbued [pervaded] with the spirit of a great ideal. This is what Mount Everest means to those who have tried to climb it.[92]

Mountaineers who climb Mt. Everest usually gain important insights about themselves and see "life for the grand thing it is."

Many modern-day climbers also feel this way about Everest. For this reason, they are willing to pay large amounts of money and take at least two months out of their lives to join an Everest expedition. Even after the 1996 disaster that took so many lives on the mountain, people still clamor to go at least partway up Everest. In 1999 more than seventeen thousand trekkers visited one of the Base Camps, and a few hundred assaulted the summit. Despite tales of physical hardship, mental stress, painful injuries, sudden death, and gruesome corpses, the lure of the mountain remains strong.

Notes

Introduction: "A Fever in the Blood"

1. Quoted in James Ramsey Ullman, *Kingdom of Adventure: Everest*. New York: William Sloane Associations, 1947, p. 352.
2. Lene Gammelgaard, *Climbing High*. New York: Perennial/HarperCollins, 1999, p. 40.
3. Quoted in Geoffrey Broughton, ed., *Climbing Everest: An Anthology*. London: Oxford University Press, 1960, pp. 64–65.
4. Reinhold Messner, *The Crystal Horizon: Everest—The First Solo Ascent*, trans. by Jill Neate and Audrey Salkeld. Seattle: Mountaineers, 1989, p. 23.
5. Anatoli Boukreev and G. Weston DeWalt, *The Climb: Tragic Ambitions on Everest*. New York: St. Martin's, 1998, p. 293.
6. Tenzing Norgay, in collaboration with James Ramsey Ullman, *Tiger of the Snows*. New York: G. P. Putnam's Sons, 1955, p. 42.

Chapter 1: Deciding When and How to Climb

7. Beck Weathers with Stephen G. Michaud, *Left for Dead: My Journey Home from Everest*. New York: Villard, 2000, p. 5.
8. Quoted in Broughton, *Climbing Everest*, p. 20.
9. Norgay, *Tiger of the Snows*, p. 161.
10. Norgay, *Tiger of the Snows*, pp. 8–9.
11. Gammelgaard, *Climbing High*, p. 63.

Chapter 2: Outfitting an Expedition

12. Ullman, *Kingdom of Adventure*, pp. 21–22.
13. Quoted in James Ramsey Ullman, *Americans on Everest: The Official Account of the Ascent Led by Norman G. Dyhrenfurth*. Philadelphia: J. B. Lippincott, 1964, p. 351.
14. Messner, *The Crystal Horizon*, p. 158.
15. Gammelgaard, *Climbing High*, p. 84.
16. Quoted in Clint Willis, ed., *High: Stories of Survival from Everest and K2*. New York: Thunder's Mouth and Balliett & Fitzgerald, 1999, pp. 239–40.
17. Quoted in Willis, *High*, pp. 260–61.
18. Sir Edmund Hillary, *View from the Summit: The Remarkable Memoir by the First Person to Conquer Everest*. New York: Pocket Books, 1999, pp. 73–74.
19. Weathers with Michaud, *Left for Dead*, p. 19.
20. Norgay, *Tiger of the Snows*, p. 41.

Chapter 3: Individual Preparations

21. Quoted in Boukreev and DeWalt, *The Climb*, p. 5.
22. Quoted in Ullman, *Kingdom of Adventure*, pp. 215–16.
23. Quoted in Broughton, *Climbing Everest*, p. 76.
24. Charles Houston, *Going Higher: Oxygen, Man, and Mountains*. Seattle: Mountaineers, 1998, p. 152.
25. Gammelgaard, *Climbing High*, pp. 68–69.
26. Houston, *Going Higher*, pp. 102–103.
27. Gammelgaard, *Climbing High*, pp. 23–24.
28. Weathers with Michaud, *Left for Dead*, pp. 46–47.
29. Matt Dickinson, *The Other Side of Everest: Climbing the North Face Through the Killer Storm*. New York: Random House, 1999, p. 30.
30. Quoted in Boukreev and DeWalt, *The Climb*, p. 47.
31. Ullman, *Americans on Everest*, p. 76.

Chapter 4: From Katmandu to Base Camp

32. Dickinson, *The Other Side of Everest*, p. 50.
33. Weathers with Michaud, *Left for Dead*, p. 19.
34. Norgay, *Tiger of the Snows*, pp. 166–67.
35. Dickinson, *The Other Side of Everest*, pp. 56–57.
36. Dickinson, *The Other Side of Everest*, pp. 68–69.
37. Gammelgaard, *Climbing High*, pp. 80–81.
38. Weathers with Michaud, *Left for Dead*, p. 19.
39. Boukreev and DeWalt, *The Climb*, pp. 90–91.
40. Boukreev and DeWalt, *The Climb*, p. 69.
41. Weathers with Michaud, *Left for Dead*, p. 15.
42. Quoted in Ullman, *Americans on Everest*, p. 115.
43. Gammelgaard, *Climbing High*, pp. 88–89.

Chapter 5: Climbing the Lower Slopes

44. Dickinson, *The Other Side of Everest*, p. 81.
45. Dickinson, *The Other Side of Everest*, pp. 86–87.
46. Dickinson, *The Other Side of Everest*, p. 94.
47. Quoted in Ullman, *Kingdom of Adventure*, p. 130.
48. Messner, *The Crystal Horizon*, pp. 207–208.
49. Don Graydon and Kurt Hanson, eds., *Mountaineering: The Freedom of the Hills*. Seattle: Mountaineers, 1997, p. 280.
50. Ullman, *Americans on Everest*, p. 104.
51. Gammelgaard, *Climbing High*, pp. 93–94.
52. Quoted in Ullman, *Kingdom of Adventure*, p. 249.
53. Gammelgaard, *Climbing High*, p. 96.
54. Boukreev and DeWalt, *The Climb*, p. 273.
55. Gammelgaard, *Climbing High*, p. 113.
56. Quoted in Broughton, *Climbing Everest*, pp. 44–45.
57. Dickinson, *The Other Side of Everest*, p. 101.
58. Jan Morris, *Coronation Everest: Eyewitness Dispatches from the Historic Hillary Climb*. Short Hills, NJ: Burford Books, 2000, pp. 69–70.
59. Morris, *Coronation Everest*, pp. 69–70.
60. Dickinson, *The Other Side of Everest*, p. 64.

Chapter 6: In the Death Zone

61. Dickinson, *The Other Side of Everest*, p. 170.
62. Quoted in Broughton, *Climbing Everest*, pp. 44–45.
63. Quoted in Willis, *High*, pp. 243–44.
64. Messner, *The Crystal Horizon*, p. 239.
65. Quoted in Broughton, *Climbing Everest*, p. 104.
66. Weathers with Michaud, *Left for Dead*, p. 30.
67. Hillary, *View from the Summit*, p. 298.
68. Quoted in Broughton, *Climbing Everest*, p. 48.
69. Quoted in Willis, *High*, p. 70.
70. Weathers with Michaud, *Left for Dead*, pp. 31–32.
71. Jon Krakauer, *Into Thin Air: A Personal Account of the Mount Everest Disaster*. New York: Villard Books, 1997, pp. 179–80.
72. Messner, *The Crystal Horizon*, p. 214.
73. Quoted in Gammelgaard, *Climbing High*, p. 24.
74. Dickinson, *The Other Side of Everest*, p. 193.
75. Quoted in Willis, *High*, p. 73.
76. Hillary, *View from the Summit*, p. 14.

77. Ullman, *Americans on Everest*, p. 187.

Chapter 7: Celebration and Descent

78. Quoted in Willis, *High*, p. 77.
79. Dickinson, *The Other Side of Everest*, p. 215.
80. Krakauer, *Into Thin Air*, pp. 180–81.
81. Weathers with Michaud, *Left for Dead*, p. 38.
82. Dickinson, *The Other Side of Everest*, pp. 218–19.
83. Quoted in Krakauer, *Into Thin Air*, p. 185.
84. Krakauer, *Into Thin Air*, p. 193.
85. Quoted in Broughton, *Climbing Everest*, p. 74.
86. Quoted in Boukreev and DeWalt, *The Climb*, p. 261.
87. Quoted in Boukreev and DeWalt, *The Climb*, p. 201.
88. Krakauer, *Into Thin Air*, p. 191.
89. Krakauer, *Into Thin Air*, p. 192.
90. Quoted in Dickinson, *The Other Side of Everest*, p. 128.
91. Krakauer, *Into Thin Air*, p. 195.
92. Quoted in Ullman, *Kingdom of Adventure*, p. 384.

For Further Reading

David Breashears and Audrey Salkeld, *Last Climb: The Legendary Everest Expeditions of George Mallory*. Washington, DC: National Geographic, 1999. Amply illustrated, this book focuses on the expeditions of George Mallory and discusses his disappearance on Everest in 1924.

Peter Firstbrook, *Lost on Everest: The Search for Mallory and Irvine*. Chicago: Contemporary Books, 1999. Firstbrook talks about the 1999 Mallory and Irvine Research Expedition, which sought to find the bodies of the two climbers—and succeeded in finding Mallory—and offers theories regarding what happened to them.

Mark Pfetzer and Jack Galvin, *Within Reach: My Everest Story*. New York: Puffin Books, 1998. In 1996, sixteen-year-old Pfetzer became the youngest person to attempt to climb Everest's summit. In this book for young adults, he discusses the failure of this attempt and talks about the importance of mountaineering in his life.

Sir Francis Younghusband, *The Epic of Mount Everest*. New York: Longmans, Green, 1924. This work is a classic of mountaineering literature. It is actually composed of edited versions of three books—*The Reconnaissance, 1921; The Assault on Mount Everest, 1922;* and *The Fight for Everest, 1924*—which recount the full story of the 1920s expeditions.

Works Consulted

Anatoli Boukreev and G. Weston DeWalt, *The Climb: Tragic Ambitions on Everest*. New York: St. Martin's, 1998. Russian climber Anatoli Boukreev describes his rescue of several climbers during a 1996 Everest storm as well as the events leading up to the disaster.

Geoffrey Broughton, ed., *Climbing Everest: An Anthology*. London: Oxford University Press, 1960. This slim volume offers excerpts from the written works of several Everest climbers.

Earl Denman, *Alone to Everest*. London: Collins, 1954. Denman describes his attempt to climb Everest by himself in 1947, a time when no permits to climb were being granted.

Matt Dickinson, *The Other Side of Everest: Climbing the North Face Through the Killer Storm*. New York: Random House, 1999. This American adventure filmmaker describes his experiences climbing the north side of Everest in 1996—when several people were killed on the mountain— while making a movie.

Lene Gammelgaard, *Climbing High*. New York: Perennial/HarperCollins, 1999. Gammelgaard describes her experiences becoming the first woman from Denmark to reach Everest's summit, an event that took place shortly before a deadly storm struck the mountain.

Don Graydon and Kurt Hanson, eds., *Mountaineering: The Freedom of the Hills*. Seattle: Mountaineers, 1997. This thick volume offers a great deal of information about how to pursue the sport of mountaineering, including descriptions of supplies and climbing techniques.

Sir Edmund Hillary, *View from the Summit: The Remarkable Memoir by the First Person to Conquer Everest*. New York: Pocket Books, 1999. Sir Hillary recalls his experiences on Everest in 1953, telling how he became the first man to reach its peak.

Charles Houston, *Going Higher: Oxygen, Man, and Mountains*. Seattle: Mountaineers, 1998. Houston discusses altitude sickness and the way climbers adjust to Everest's height.

Sir John Hunt, *The Conquest of Everest*. Garden City, NY: International Collectors Library, 1953. The leader of the 1953 expedition describes his experiences in coordinating and commanding the first successful summit assault.

Jon Krakauer, *Into Thin Air: A Personal Account of the Mount Everest Disaster*. New York: Villard Books, 1997. Nonfiction writer Jon Krakauer went on a 1996 Everest expedition on assignment from *Outside* magazine; this is his account of the disaster that occurred on the mountain that year. Although highly readable, it has been criticized as inaccurate and/or misleading by some of the other mountaineers on Everest at the time, most notably Anatoli Boukreev.

Reinhold Messner, *The Crystal Horizon: Everest—The First Solo Ascent*. Trans. Jill Neate and Audrey Salkeld. Seattle: Mountaineers, 1989. Messner tells about his experiences becoming the first person to summit Everest alone; he also discusses the sport of mountaineering in general and mountaineering on Everest in particular.

Jan Morris, *Coronation Everest: Eyewitness Dispatches from the Historic Hillary*

Climb. Short Hills, NJ: Burford Books, 2000. Morris was a journalist who accompanied the 1953 Everest expedition to write about its exploits for the *Times* newspaper of London; this work, which contains a detailed account of the expedition, was originally published in 1958, when the author was using the name James Morris.

Tenzing Norgay, in collaboration with James Ramsey Ullman, *Tiger of the Snows*. New York: G. P. Putnam's Sons, 1955. The autobiography of Tenzing Norgay, who, with Edmund Hillary in 1953, became the first person to reach Everest's summit. Norgay discusses other climbs as well and touches on the controversy regarding exactly which man first put his foot on the summit.

Sherry B. Ortner, *Life and Death on Mount Everest: Sherpas and Himalayan Mountaineering*. Princeton, NJ: Princeton University Press, 1999. Ortner offers a detailed examination of Sherpa life and culture.

Woodrow Wilson Sayre, *Four Against Everest*. Englewood Cliffs, NJ: Prentice-Hall, 1964. Sayre tells of his failed 1962 expedition, during which he sneaked into Tibet without a permit and with only four expedition members.

James Ramsey Ullman, *Americans on Everest: The Official Account of the Ascent Led by Norman G. Dyhrenfurth*. Philadelphia: J. B. Lippincott, 1964. This thick volume offers detailed information about the successful 1963 American Everest expedition.

————, *Kingdom of Adventure: Everest*. New York: William Sloane Associations, 1947. This book discusses Everest expeditions of the 1920s and 1930s, offering a large number of quotes from expedition members.

Beck Weathers with Stephen G. Michaud, *Left for Dead: My Journey Home from Everest*. New York: Villard, 2000. Weathers describes his experiences surviving a deadly storm on Everest in 1996 as well as his feelings about the sport of mountaineering.

Clint Willis, ed., *High: Stories of Survival from Everest and K2*. New York: Thunder's Mouth and Balliett & Fitzgerald, 1999. This book offers excerpts from mountaineers' writings about their experiences on the two highest mountains in the world, Everest and K2.

Index

Picture Credits

Cover Photo: National Geographic Image Collection/B. Bishop

Archive Photos/Hulton Getty Picture Library, 35, 38

Corbis/Michael Freeman, 47

Corbis/Hulton-Deutsch Collection, 10

Corbis/Craig Lovell, 49

Corbis/Dave Samuel Robbins, 20

Corbis/Galen Rowell, 9, 13, 14, 19, 39, 61, 62, 69, 70

Sipa Press/*Ft. Worth Star*/Deavers, 90

Woodfin Camp & Associates/Neal Beidleman, 18, 25, 28, 31, 41, 44, 46, 55, 57, 63, 65, 75, 78, 82, 85

Woodfin Camp & Associates/Scott Fischer, 15, 27, 34, 67, 81, 88, 93

Woodfin Camp & Associates/Caroline Mackenzie, 52

About the Author

Patricia D. Netzley received a bachelor's degree in English from the University of California at Los Angeles (UCLA). After graduation she worked as an editor at the UCLA Medical Center, where she produced hundreds of medical articles, speeches, and pamphlets. Her books for Lucent's Mystery Library series include UFOs, The Curse of King Tut, Witches, and Haunted Houses. Her hobbies are weaving, knitting, and needlework. She and her husband, Raymond, live in southern California with their children, Matthew, Sarah, and Jacob.